THREE DECADES
OF LILY

THREE DECADES

OF LILY

Diane C. Smyth

Library of Congress Control Number: 2010906083
ISBN: Hardcover   978-1-4500-9120-6
                          Softcover   978-1-4500-9119-0
                          Ebook   978-1-4500-9121-3

To order additional copies of this book, contact:
Xlibris Corporation
1-888-795-4274
www.Xlibris.com
Orders@Xlibris.com
80360

To my Dad whose death taught me strength in written words.
To my Mom who is the most incredible woman I know. You give unconditional love and encouragement. Without you both my gift would not exist.

To my sons David and Danny. I love you both very much. You are my heart. Always remember that with patience and persistence, all dreams are possible!

To four incredible women who I have the privilege to call my best friends, who never gave up on me and who inspire the ladies of *Quei Forti*.

I love you all!

CHAPTER 1

It was a crisp winter morning in Arlington. The dew was present on the blades of grass. Today was one of those days in your life when you wish you didn't have to live it. Saying goodbye is hard, it is heart wrenching, it is final.

Five layers deep family and friends stood at the burial site to bid their final farewell. Tears were flowing as the geese flew overhead marking the gray sky's exit into spring. It wouldn't be long now.

The four women stood shoulder to shoulder, more leaning than standing to keep from falling down. The echo of the minister resounded softly in their heads as they tried to take in why they were there. "God, give me strength," they all thought, "strength to get through the next minute." They couldn't think any farther ahead than one minute at a time. It was just too much to take in, too much to believe. They kept hoping if they closed their eyes tight enough when they opened again, it would all be a horrible mistake; a nightmare.

"It's time," she whispered. "Everyone else is gone and we can't put this off any longer."

They joined hands to proceed to the coffin before it was lowered into the ground. One . . . two . . . three . . . four . . . five, they all fell atop the coffin; a rainbow of lilies, full of color indicative of new life. One might say it was the beginning of new life for her; everlasting life with no more pain, no more threats and no more fears.

They walked away arm-in-arm, tears streaming down their faces knowing it was the end for her, for the five of them, for *Quei Forti*. They got into the limousine waiting to take them back to the City.

"Driver, can you drop us at *The Gathering* please, 17th and L?" she requested.

The ride from Arlington to Washington was riddled with silence. Words don't ever seem to do any good at a time like this. So they retreated into their own thoughts and tried to recall the vibrancy that was always part of who she was in life. They owed her a tribute to befit the life they shared. They needed to replace the sadness with the laughter of her soul that they'd all come to know and love. She was the glue that held them together. She was their voice of reason when they wanted to go off half-cocked, leaping before thinking and acting with caution abandoned. *Quei Forti* would never be the same. They lost the strongest link in the chain and now had to learn how to rebuild.

The opening of the car door pulled them back to reality. "*The Gathering*, ladies. Will you be requiring my services anymore today?"

"No John," she declined. "Thank you for your kindness. We can make it on our own from here."

"Hello ladies," greeted the bartender as they headed to their favorite spot in the back of the pub. "I've been expecting you today. Take a seat and I'll send your drinks to the table."

She leaned in to place a slight kiss on his cheek. "The flowers were beautiful, Mickey. Thank you."

"Everyone here loved her, too. It's a sad day," he sorrowfully acknowledged.

They gathered around their favorite table in the back by the jukebox. She loved music and needed to be close to the songs. A small fortune was spent in the jukebox because the mood had to be high and the beat had to be up. They all stared at the empty chair where she would have been sitting; another reminder that their lives were about to change. Nothing would ever be the same.

"Hey, do you guys remember one of the first times we came here, the night Mickey was trying out a new band and their lead singer was late for the first set?" she reminded. "She felt so bad for the band she jumped up on stage and filled in until their singer finally arrived."

Laughter sprang from each of them as they remembered her nervousness. Her voice was cracking until she looked over at them and gained the confidence she needed. Then the most beautiful sounds emerged from her mouth as she settled down to please the crowd.

"And do you remember . . ."

CHAPTER 2

Cassie Davis

Cassie Davis spent many cold winters sneaking into New York's *The Tent* to catch a glimpse of the gorgeous fashions gracing the sleek, slender figures of the most beautiful models from all around the world. The Promenade, The Salon, The Showroom—each one filled with excitement, glitter and wonder.

Every year Cassie would ditch school for one day during Fashion Week to chase her dream. School officials and her parents always caught her but it didn't matter because this was going to be her life and she would one day own this show. In her heart she knew the only way to make that a reality was to learn the details of how it all worked, absorb it all, and become a sponge. It was a small price to pay to be grounded for a week or two compared to the value of what she took away from the event every year. The people, the hair, the hats, the style, the grace, and the pressure—it was all so wonderful!

Roslyn, New York, a village of approximately twenty-five hundred people, was located on the North Shore of Long Island in Nassau County. Cassie lived in Roslyn with her mother and younger brother Joel since her birth in 1968. It wasn't always the three of them.

Mr. Davis, a New York City fireman, was killed in a tragic car accident on his way to work on a cold November morning. It was supposed to be his day off and plans were made for the family to spend it together. A call came from the station that one of the guys on shift had a family emergency and the company was short a ladder man. That was the end of the day off and the end of a happy family.

Cassie worked hard during high school to become a seamstress. She pondered every fashion magazine she could get her hands on. She so desperately wanted to see one of her own designs gliding down the runway. But all of her schoolwork and efforts only reinforced that she had no artistic ability for designing. It was time to regroup, evaluate the situation and focus on the strengths she did own.

Parties were always the popular happening for high school students. Being able to throw a soiree that people actually attended was something different. The competitiveness that brought out the worst in most people brought out the best in Cassie.

Janet Harding was Cassie's sidekick during junior high and high school. They were inseparable except when it came to fashion. Cassie loved the scene and Janet wanted nothing to do with it.

"Those mannequins are coat hangers with legs," Janet bashed.

Cassie knew she could not sway Janet from her opinion. They debated this topic for years and to continue was only beating a dead horse. But it wasn't a problem for their friendship. Cassie respected Janet's opinion and for all Janet's criticism and colorful characterizations, she respected Cassie's right to have a differing one.

Cassie had a theory that if you were the best at something that everyone else wanted and offered it as a service to someone who was, for the most part, snubbed throughout most of their adolescent life, that person would suddenly be the hottest ticket in town. She also believed that the acclaim attributed to the person offering that service would allow that besting to lead her right to the front door of success. She decided to test her theory.

Janet was never one of the more popular girls in school. In fact, the birthday party she had back in the seventh grade was the last one ever because only three of the twelve friends she invited showed up. It was a disappointment for Janet, but she always understood she was cast out of most circles in the eyes of her classmates.

Cassie was going to plan Janet's coming out party. It took some convincing for Janet to agree to be a guinea pig but she knew from the moment the words crossed Cassie's lips that she would do anything to help her friend. It might even help her, too.

Even though the party was held at the local Moose Lodge, it still impressed the more admired population of the senior class because it was a public venue and not a house bash. Cassie put together a fascinating party and everyone that came to it raved about the flamboyance and excitement.

When all was said and done, Cassie's theory proved correct. Janet's quiet little homebody world was turned upside down by a completely congested social life. It took some getting used to but Janet was enjoying her newfound fame.

Cassie, on the other hand, was not quite as popular in the social standings but she could not keep up with the number of people wanting her to plan their graduation parties. A lesson learned for Cassie: be careful what you wish for because you might get so much of it that you don't have time to enjoy the festivities yourself.

She found it. She found her niche and was taking it all the way to the top. Cassie wanted to be a party planner, keep her eyes on the prize and one day be the organizer for Fashion Week!

♦　♦　♦　♦　♦　♦　♦　♦

College was more of a debut for Cassie even though that ship set sail back in high school. She took all the right classes and studied all the current fashion trends, hot spots and designers. She knew all the top players and made sure to keep abreast of all that was hip and exciting. In order to achieve success she not only had to know all the right things, she had to make all the right connections and build a name for herself in this world she had truly come to love.

She continued her party planning business to help with tuition and school expenses on a much more advanced level. She took some of her college money and invested it in the business thinking it would yield a nice return and no one would be the wiser.

It didn't take long before word got out around campus. Anyone who was anyone at school and wanted to throw the party of the year had to hire Cassie Davis for the job. She became known as the SOURCE—Specialist Of Upper Renowned Classy Events.

Her first big break came when she organized a party for Jenna Stark's twenty-first birthday. Jenna's dad, Ben Stark, was a big shot on Wall Street who loved to shower his daughter with extravagant parties and gifts. Ben believed that since he held a high profile position in the Manhattan social circles, it was only befitting that Jenna be as much in the spotlight as he'd come to be. Ben had many contacts that could easily plan and organize Jenna's party and it would be an event equal to no other. But Jenna insisted it be the Source.

Cassie was used to working with a budget of a couple thousand dollars when she planned her parties. Organizing this party was an opportunity to see what she could pull together with an unlimited budget. Jenna was an Art History major so Cassie thought it would be fun to incorporate those interests into the party theme.

The *Metropolitan Museum of Art* was one of Jenna's favorite places. The idea to transform her father's lavish 2-level penthouse into the museum's principal deities in the Greek pantheon started to take on a life of its own. Obviously Cassie did not have twelve rooms to dress so she settled on five of the more commonly known gods to act as servants to the beautiful Jenna for a day.

Athena, the patron goddess of Athens, served as the center point from which the rest of the party expanded. Being the patroness of weaving and carpentry, the foyer was accented with goatskin rugs, woven baskets and a statue of Athena in full armor with a snaky fringe, a helmet and a spear. Behind Athena stood a small olive tree and on her left hand an owl. Her grand stature greeted each guest in celebrity style.

Zeus, the god of the sky and the father of all other gods, had a room designed around the ox and the oak tree. Being most associated with weather and a thunderbolt as his main attributes, flashes of lightning were witnessed as claps of thunder and falling rain were heard softly echoing throughout the room.

Apollo, the son of Zeus often shown with an ancient Greek wooden musical instrument called a cithara, stood proud as the god of music and prophecy. His sanctuary was considered the center of the universe so it was only fitting that his room housed Hermes, the disc jockey. Lining the wall on the far side of the room were two incredibly crafted ice sculptures of a swan and a dolphin, both sacred to Apollo. A karaoke machine was available for enjoyment to replicate Apollo's direction of the choir of the Muses when the disc jockey elected to take a break.

Artemis, Apollo's twin sister, was best known as a virgin goddess of the wilderness, patroness of the hunt, and a goddess of fertility and childbirth. It was mesmerizing to envision the room's blend of the darkened sky bursting with stars and the glow of the distant moon. Unicorns and wolves accented the room to capture the mood of an evening hunt.

Last but not least was the shrine of Aphrodite, the goddess of love, beauty and sexual rapture. Her statue was adorned with the finest gold ornaments and lavish jewels. She was clothed in a golden girdle with woven magic that Greek myth maintains made her irresistible to men when she wore it. Naturally, her room was aglow with candlelight and a faint heart-rending aria in opera could be heard in the background. As Aphrodite was known for being born of the sea, a champagne fountain flowed in the center of the room. Off on several side tables were flowing fountains of various sizes radiating the finest chocolates and cheeses for the guests' dipping pleasure.

Everyone was captivated by the sacred décor.

Cassie was quite pleased with herself. Everything was coming together nicely and Jenna was thrilled. This was "the" party to beat this year!

The Pièce de résistance was the food. The caterer, Marcella Leone, was known for her exceptional food and outstanding presentation. Once Marcella agreed to put the final touches on an event, she made sure the party was a memorable and spectacular occasion. Cassie was honored that Marcella agreed to be part of Jenna's celebration, which entailed serving over two hundred fifty guests. Not only was their collaboration guaranteeing the party's success, Cassie stood to gain many new high society clients.

Ben Stark could really work a room! As he crossed the atrium toward Cassie, she admired his striking physical appearance and dominating personality that easily adapted to the calm, sensitive, caring and thoughtful man who she'd come to respect in the last few months. He stood just over six feet tall with blue eyes, premature salt and pepper hair, and a well-defined, toned physique. His pleasing physical features hid the fact he was a man approaching fifty.

Cassie secretly wondered if this dashing older gentleman saw her as the woman she was becoming. She sported a new stylish short blonde bob with long side bangs framing her cheeks and accenting her bright blue eyes. As a woman just at 5'4" she chose a solid black petite fitted evening dress, streamlined to elongate her body, and pulling it together with a pair of four inch heels to appear taller. The ensemble was fitted, flattering and offered the most amazing effect!

"Judging by the look on Jenna's face, I would say you earned every penny of your commission Ms. Davis," he praised. "Why don't we tie up loose ends so we can relax and enjoy the rest of the evening? Please come with me to my study and I'll get you a check."

Cassie knew she was blushing. "I'm glad you're happy with the festivities. I had so much fun planning this party. It almost seems unfair to charge you for my time. But since you are happy with how it all turned out, I would be grateful if you would refer me to your friends in the future." Cassie knew a good plug from Ben Stark would go a long way in ascending her ambition ladder.

They entered the study and Ben motioned for Cassie to take a seat in front of his desk. "I'll be right back," he said. After pushing a button under his desk, the bookcase behind him separated leaving an opening into an adjoining room.

"I left my checkbook in the other room last night when I was working," he apprised. "Please excuse me."

As Ben disappeared into the "secret room" Cassie couldn't help but feed her curiosity. She walked around the back of the desk to peek inside.

"Come in," Ben invited. "This is my get away zone when I've had a stressful day and need to release some tension."

He walked over to the stereo and flipped the power button. The sound exploded from the speakers and caught Cassie off-guard. He quickly turned the volume down and extended his apologies once again.

"Well now you know my secret," he confessed. "I like to turn the music up loud when I work in here. It helps me tune out distractions. I'm sure that sounds a little adolescent, but I trust you can keep my confidence," he teased with a boyish grin as he handed Cassie her check. "Of course, when I play it really loud, I close the door because the room is soundproof. Would you like to hear how loud it goes?"

Cassie was having fun bonding with Ben. She walked to the door and pushed the button on the wall. "I guess we all have a little adolescent in us," she replied as she gestured for him to crank it up.

Within seconds, the floor and walls were vibrating from the bass and both she and Ben sat down on the couch to listen for a few minutes before returning to the party.

"Close your eyes," he shouted. "It helps you feel the music."

Cassie did as he suggested. She was enjoying herself tremendously and releasing the pressure from the months' of work leading up to this night. It was a consuming fantasia. Unexpectedly, she felt his lips touch hers. Her eyes sprang open from shear surprise as she pulled away and stretched back from his intimidating presence. He obviously did not get the hint because Ben took her face between his hands and began to part her lips driving his tongue into her mouth. Cassie pushed him off with all the strength she could gather but he was too strong. She pulled her face away from his hands and begged him, not only with the frightened look in her eyes, but with the words she mouthed in competition with the deafening music, not to do this. Ben Stark was not hearing or seeing any of it.

He leaned over and whispered in Cassie's ear, "I've paid for it all; the party, my daughter's happiness and you. Jenna has told me all about you. You are ambitious. I know your dreams and what you hope to achieve. I can make it all come true for you, but first you have to decide how important they really are because I can just as easily squash them.

♦ ♦ ♦ ♦ ♦ ♦ ♦ ♦

With knees shaking and buckling underneath the weight of her tiny frame, Cassie climbed into the cab. Her hands were trembling uncontrollably and she was grateful for the doorman's assistance. The cab pulled away from the curb and Ben Stark's penthouse faded in the distance.

It was unthinkable. It was inconceivable. She was flabbergasted. How did she not see this coming? Was she really so naïve to fall for a deceptive move like entering a "secret" room belonging to a rich and powerful man? Cassie was uncertain what disturbed her more, the fact that this man was so confident he could breach her this way in a house with two hundred fifty guests or that she was awakened by the exploit and was now consumed with anticipation for an encore.

What a lucrative collaboration Ben Stark would be.

CHAPTER 3

Sheila Marmion

Sensitivity, emotion, and insecurity. Sheila Marmion carried them like badges of honor as a child. She was one of three girls born to Edward and Samantha Marmion in Northern California.

The oldest daughter Anne was an accomplished member of the Honor Society. She held a grade point average higher than the number of combined dates Sheila had in the last year. It didn't hurt that Anne was tall, slender and had the most beautiful long hair, black as the night void of stars and silky enough to catch the reflection of the moon on the water.

Kitty, the middle child, was full of energy and love of life. She was extremely popular and there was hardly a Friday night that she didn't have a date with the captain of the football team or the most valuable player on the basketball team. She had her own strengths. Kitty was a gifted musician. Many said she played like a cool gentle breeze on a hot summer night: welcome and refreshing. She knew her way around a tennis court, too.

Sheila, the youngest daughter, worked twice as hard for less recognition except when she wrote her stories. She spent hours alone composing and dreaming of a future with success and acknowledgement. She wanted to be on the New York Times Best Seller List. To that end, Sheila was not the most social of animals. She was shy and introverted; a loner who most thought peculiar because of her independent nature. She, too, was tall and slender with a smooth solid hairline that fell to her waistline, ideal to capture the essence of her gorgeous blue eyes and red spiral curls.

The Marmion girls grew up in Colusa, a small town outside Sacramento. The population was barely more than 5,000 and everyone knew everyone else's business. Edward and Samantha owned the butcher store on the corner of Railroad and Main. This was not a good thing in Sheila's opinion. The townspeople would come into the store for their meat and thirty minutes later her parents knew everything that was going on around town. A private life was unexpected and near impossible in Colusa. One day this would all be a faded, distant memory when she moved away to San Francisco.

Sheila enjoyed her down time. When she wasn't doing chores around the house or helping out in the store, she was out under the oak tree working diligently to compose. She was very ambitious when it came to her stories and blocked out the world to go to that place where her imagination ran wild. Her stories were often so vivid and detailed that even Sheila's parents wondered if they were fact or fiction. People were in awe of her literature. In this domain, Anne and Kitty couldn't hold a candle to her accomplishments. Sheila got used to her sisters excelling in everything else because what she did far outweighed their combined achievements in school, sports and music. At least she believed it did. Unfortunately for Sheila, she was not recognized as often as Anne and Kitty but she was patient knowing her day would come.

♦ ♦ ♦ ♦ ♦ ♦ ♦ ♦

San Francisco State University—one of the leading urban educational venues in the Bay Area—was Sheila's home for the next 4 years. At last count, the student population was upwards of 30,000 and to most that would have been horrifying, especially a shy, quiet introvert like Sheila. But she knew this was a necessary step in her plan. She formed new alliances with a few close friends and professors and donned fashion in purple and gold. Just like the characters she fabricated, this was a chance to create a new life; a blank sheet of paper waiting for the words to appear, to fill up the page and have it develop into a story before her eyes. It was new, exciting and replete with endless possibilities for Sheila.

Her chosen major was a Bachelor of Arts in Journalism—news-editorial and magazine. Her first year's classes were as expected; lectures during the day and studying every night. Sheila declined most invitations for partying. Although it never really was her scene, it was challenging to keep saying no when everyone else was having so much fun. She kept her eyes on the prize and spent most of her time studying to make honor roll.

The second and third year proved more difficult. The assignments were intense and the amount of time Sheila was spending alone was adding to the stress of maintaining her 4.0 GPA. Although she did not want to stray from her good grades, she was lonely and wished she had taken more opportunities to appreciate the social aspect of college life. However, she did as she programmed herself to do and pushed those thoughts out of her mind for now.

Early on in her senior year her roommate and best friend, Trina Knapp, begged her to come along to a Halloween party. Trina had her eyes on a guy from a neighboring college and heard he was having a party. It was her chance to arrange an introduction but she didn't want to go alone. She wouldn't have hounded Sheila so much if it weren't already so late and everyone else had plans.

As usual Sheila declined enouncing, "I have too much work for tomorrow's classes to go to some silly costume party."

Trina assured her they did not have to wear costumes and continued to relentlessly apply peer pressure for over an hour. After a sufficient amount of groveling on Trina's part, Sheila caved and agreed to go.

"But we must be home by midnight," pleaded Sheila. "I have a big test in the morning that I can't screw it up. Got it, Tree?"

"Shit, yeah! That works for me. I have a term paper for my English Lit class that I need to finish in the morning anyway. Yeah, that works for me," Trina agreed.

As they drove up to the house, Sheila thought it was amazing the cops hadn't shut down the party. Cars were strewn all over the front yard, music was blaring from inside the house, and Sheila got a sudden queasy feeling in her gut. Her better judgment was telling her this wasn't a good idea. A party this out of control rarely ends well. But she promised Trina and it would be better to go inside together than to let Trina go in alone.

Everyone inside was clad in costume garb. Sheila was uncomfortable being around so many people whose faces were covered with masks. It didn't help that Trina and Sheila were not wearing costumes, which made them look like the misfits.

"A drink would help now, don't you think?" Trina suggested.

"Tree, I'm not sure about this," Sheila cautioned. "There are so many people here. How are you going to find Mark? Parties and big crowds just don't do anything for me, other than make my skin crawl," she added. "I don't mind the occasional family backyard barbeque, but when the number of people at the party is larger than the number of days in a month, hell a week, the hair on the back of my neck stands up and the walls start to close in."

"Okay then let's go out back," Trina offered as a solution to her uneasiness. "I think there's a pool out there. We can sit and dangle our feet while we people watch. You used to like doing that. I'll bet there's a lot of disguised weirdoes here tonight."

"Yeah, but is it the disguise that makes them weird or are they weirdoes by nature?" Sheila questioned. "Alright I'll go. But first you have to promise not to disappear on me. We came to this free-for-all together and we leave together. Agreed?"

"Agreed, now let's go have fun," Trina urged.

She grabbed Sheila by the hand and led her through the hallways to the back of the house. Neither one of them knew exactly where they were going but if you walk a straight line away from the front of the house, chances are you'll reach the back. They did!

The mood in the yard was resonant. It would appear that the more mature students were out back and the wilder, less restrained group was inside. You would think the host of the party would prefer it the other way around but who knew where he was at this point.

Trina and Sheila found a couple of empty lounge chairs alongside the pool. It was an unexpected mild evening and not a cloud in the sky or sign of fog. Sheila noticed two guys on the other side of the pool who must have been talking about them because they kept glancing their way. She managed to avoid eye contact and carry on a conversation with Trina but soon lost that battle when out of the corner of her eye she saw them get up and head their way.

The tall blonde addressed them first. "Good evening ladies. I notice you don't have a drink. Can I get you something from the bar? Oh, by the way, I'm Sean and this is Barry."

"Hello ladies." With a tip of his cowboy hat, Barry managed a wink.

"Hello," Sheila began, "I'm Sheila and this is Trina."

"Nice to meet you," Trina chimed in.

"As I was saying, can I get you ladies a drink from the bar?" Sean asked again.

"Beer would be fine," Sheila accepted.

Sean went to the bar for the drinks. Barry made himself comfortable at the foot of Sheila's lounger regardless of the fact that her legs were stretched out. If she hadn't moved them as quickly as she did, he would have sat on them.

"Barry," interrupted Trina, "I take it you're supposed to be a cowboy?"

"Yes, ma'am and we cowboys definitely know how to treat a lady," he bragged.

Sheila couldn't believe it. "Does this guy really believe those lines he's sputtering?" she thought to herself. She wanted to blurt out "loser", but managed to restrain herself.

Trina resumed, "Do you know where I can find Mark?"

"If you mean our host," answered Barry, "I think he's upstairs in the den with some people playing pool. The house is open. Go on up if you'd like."

"Thanks. I'm not really comfortable roaming around his house since we've never actually met. I was invited to this party by a mutual friend and just wanted to say hi," she confessed.

Although that technically was a lie, it really didn't matter since this was an open house party anyway.

"No problem. When Sean gets back, the four of us can go upstairs and I will introduce you as personal friends of mine," he suggested.

As Trina was accepting Barry's invitation, Sean returned with the beer and they all headed into the house to find Mark. The girls were genuinely impressed with the elaborate carvings on the wooden handrails and paintings lining the spiral staircase. At the top was a long, intimidating hallway with more artwork nestled between the doors, many doors.

Halfway down the corridor Sean stopped and opened a door. Sheila had never seen a room that big. Apparently, several of the doors in the hallway opened up into this room. It was huge. There were two pool tables, dartboards, and a drink ledge that ran along three walls, a bar, and several pinball machines.

"This might turn out to be a fun party after all," Sheila whispered to Trina.

There were about a dozen other people in the room, mostly men, but Sheila did see a couple of women. Barry made the introductions to Mark who, as Trina had hoped, took an instant liking to her. Sheila nudged her as a reminder of their arrangement to stay together. She nodded in agreement and off she went with Mark to the bar, leaving Sheila with Sean and Barry.

Sheila had never picked up a pool cue in her life. No one was more surprised than she was to learn her skill came naturally. The mirrored wall lining the room showed a pleasing reflection of her technique. As the night grew later, Sheila relaxed and was having fun. In fact, her usually demure behavior was more liberated and carefree. She was happier than she'd been in a long time.

Sheila glanced at the clock above the bar noting the time as eleven p.m. The hands seemed blurry and she was having difficulty maintaining her balance. Looking around for Trina she grew dizzy and unfocused. Confused and scared she sought out Barry's help.

♦ ♦ ♦ ♦ ♦ ♦ ♦ ♦

Sheila awoke to the sun pouring through the window of her dorm room. Her head was pounding and she felt groggy and exhausted.

Trina came running to her bed, "Oh thank goodness you're awake. I've been trying to get you up for hours. You missed your class. I've been so worried. I finished my English Lit paper but skipped the class because I thought something was wrong with you. What happed to you last night? Did you take drugs or something?"

"Take? What are you talking about? Why is my head pounding?" she asked. "Please make the pain go away."

"Sheila, we couldn't find you for hours last night," Trina informed her. "When we did, it was almost two o'clock in the morning and you were in one of the bedrooms passed out. Sounds like someone had too much fun! Who's the lucky guy?"

"What are you talking about?" Sheila asked. "The last thing I remember is looking for you around eleven o'clock then asking Barry for help because I wanted to go home. Where you said you found me, how did I get there?"

"I don't know," Trina replied. "Maybe when you were looking for me you got tired and decided to lie down. My guess is you just overdid it on the partying without realizing how much you were drinking. For the first time since you came to this place, you had fun and were laughing. Don't over-think this. It's no big deal and we've all been where you are now, in hangover hell. You must have one helluva headache. When we found you, you weren't wearing any clothes."

"Trina," she faintly spoke, "I would not take my clothes off in a strange house. I wouldn't even drink enough to take my clothes off in a strange house. Something is not right about this whole thing. Did anything bizarre happen to you?"

"No," she replied. "But really, it's not a big deal. Overindulgence is like shit: it happens, especially when you don't get out much socially. You have bigger issues than a loss of memory right now. How are you going to deal with that test you missed today? You'd better get up and go find your professor."

◆　◆　◆　◆　◆　◆　◆　◆

The news was sudden and unexpected. It was ambiguous to say the least. Trina could not understand why Sheila would opt to graduate in December, rather than finish the year with the rest of the class. She tried to dissuade her from making this decision without first going home to discuss it with her parents, but Sheila's mind was made up. She was too excited about the job waiting for her at the San Francisco Examiner. Something about the suddenness of it all had Trina questioning the validity of her story. "Maybe I should call your parents and ask them to talk some sense into you before you do something you can't take back," threatened Trina.

"Don't even think about it," Sheila warned. "This is my business and you need to stay the hell out of it! Trina if you call my parents, I will never speak to you again as long as I live."

While away at college, Sheila grew distant from her family. She managed the obligatory trips home for the holidays but lately she even skipped some of the more important ones. Somewhere along the way, Sheila became estranged from her family; less frequent phone calls and eventually all letters stopped, too. Sheila accepted a lot of the blame because her independence caused her to keep mostly to herself. But she still felt a twinge of sadness beginning this new chapter of her life alone, or at least lonely.

She knew what her next step had to be and she believed it would be easier this way. First she had to make it through one more family holiday—Christmas.

CHAPTER 4

Sunny Gianquinto

Baltimore, Maryland—a rough place for a young girl to grow up. Although the city was shaped with museums, baseball, restaurants of diverse culture and an abundance of heritage, Sunny Gianquinto had nothing but misfortunate when it came to appreciation of such jewels. She grew up in West Baltimore where the streets were rough and the people were as friendly as you'd expect considering the crime rate and number of delinquents living among them. Almost half the houses on the block were boarded up and abandoned.

It was a mixed neighborhood of homeowners and low-income rental housing. The population was a mix of African American and Caucasian with some quite scary characters in the neighborhood.

On one of her daily walks home from school Sunny caught glimpse of a little old lady planting colorful flowers under her windows because there was no grass or trees in the front yard. Next door were a dozen delinquents hanging out on the stoop. Sunny noticed the drugs exchanging hands and heard the loud dirt bikes racing up and down the street. She looked over at the woman and shook her head. Sunny's heart went out to her. She obviously lived alone and had little control over what was happening in her own front yard.

Many residents were hopeful that one day the abandoned houses would be cleaned up. For now all Sunny could think about was getting out of this hell, even if it meant running away from it all.

Patapsco River was a major transportation route just minutes from downtown Baltimore. Sunny's dad worked in the Maritime Industrial Park as a forklift operator for long hours and short pay. Tony Gianquinto did his best to provide for his family but hardships were difficult to avoid and money was often tight.

The day Sunny came into the world was one of mixed blessings. Tony and Angela Gianguinto were ecstatic that their family was growing and looked forward to the new baby arriving.

Angela was at home when her labor started. It had been a difficult pregnancy so they were taking precautions to make sure she went to term and delivered a healthy baby. Something about these contractions felt wrong. The onset of pain was quicker and more intense than what she was told to expect. Worried that something was wrong, Angela called her neighbor and asked for a ride to the hospital, rather than wait for Tony to get home to pick her up.

Upon arriving at the emergency room, Angela was immediately taken upstairs to labor and delivery and her doctor was summoned to the hospital. After thirty minutes of Angela screaming out in pain, the nurses suspected a problem. An emergency situation was developing so they quickly paged the doctor on call.

When Tony arrived, Angela was in surgery. "I am so sorry, Mr. Gianquinto," apologized the nurse, "there was no time to wait for you. Your wife is in good hands and the babies will be just fine."

"Babies?" questioned Tony. "Are you telling me we're having twins?"

You could hear the excitement in his voice, but at the same time fear and anxiety came rushing to the surface. How was he going to feed two babies when he could barely feed himself and his wife? Just as he pushed that thought out of his mind, determined to focus on the health of his wife and children, the doctor came out of the operating room.

"Mr. Gianquinto," he stated as a matter of fact extending his hand. "We did everything we could to save them all. Unfortunately, our efforts fell short and we lost one of the babies. You have a beautiful, healthy little girl but I'm afraid your other daughter was stillborn. Your wife is in recovery and she's asking to see you."

Thinking back on that day always left a heavy heart in Tony's chest for the loss of his daughter Vivian. Each time he reflected on that wonderful yet heart-wrenching day the pain was fresh and raw. Tony and Angela told Sunny about her twin sister when she was old enough to understand.

For years Sunny could not put a finger on a recurring memory that she suspected was just a fabrication in her own mind. Once the images were validated she understood them to be an ache for her sister. The ache was stronger when she was lonely and Sunny was certain that Vivian was with her every day of her life, sometimes encouraging her to take small chances and sometimes being the voice of reason when she was not so strong.

Sunny did her best to be a good girl and obey her parents. Sometimes the other teens would ridicule her for always being the goody-goody. One chilly October day, she decided to show them that she could be defiant along with the rest of them. Designer jeans were the current fad but there was no way her parents could afford a pair. Sunny decided to steal them to just once be like the rest of the kids and blend. While the manager was not looking she grabbed two pairs of Corniche jeans, both the same size, and took them into the fitting room. Corniche jeans were designed to be skintight so the loose cotton pants Sunny was already wearing would hide the new pants underneath.

As she exited the fitting room the manager was standing near her door offering assistance with other items. Sunny handed her the second pair of jeans declining further assistance and walked toward the exit. As she was about to get away with her act of delinquency, the manager called out. From the back of store the manager could see the Corniche pant legs peeking out from under Sunny's pants.

◆ ◆ ◆ ◆ ◆ ◆ ◆ ◆

Community service sucks! Not only was Sunny going to be on permanent grounding by her parents, she had to sacrifice her free time to work at the homeless shelter.

Camille Sax, the store manager, did not want to get the police involved. When Sunny's parents came to the security office to pick her up Camille suggested an alternative. Rather than put Sunny into the system she could work off her offense. Stepping Up, a homeless shelter on Abigail Street, was in desperate need of volunteers. If

Sunny agreed to give up two months of Saturdays then Camille would consider her debt to society paid in full.

"Two months," whined Sunny. "That's not fair."

"Would you rather go to the police station and take your chances with a judge?" her dad inquired. "I think Miss Sax is being very generous. You're getting off easy and I suggest you take her offer before she changes her mind."

"Fine, I'll do it. What do I need to do?" she asked Camille.

"I'll pick you up Saturday morning at eight o'clock and take you to the shelter," Camille offered. "I volunteer in the office on the weekends so I will give you a ride home, too. You'll help out in the kitchen washing dishes or doing laundry."

"Great. Sounds just like prison." With that Sunny glanced over at her mother and saw the disappointment in her eyes. "What I meant to say was thank you for not calling the police."

A tiny grin formed on Angela's mouth but quickly faded when she realized Sunny was watching her.

"Okay kiddo. Let's go home. We still have to deal with this on a family level," her mom said as she placed her hands on Sunny's shoulders. "You're not out of the woods yet."

◆ ◆ ◆ ◆ ◆ ◆ ◆ ◆

The first month of community service passed quickly. Sunny put up with her friends' teasing about getting caught but deep down she was relieved. She didn't want to be known for stealing and she was afraid it would get worse if she got away with it. She wanted to be different than the other kids in the neighborhood, the troublemakers. They were on every corner.

Camille wasn't so bad either. Sunny found it easy to confide in Camille about her dream to one day make it big anywhere away from Baltimore. When asked how she was planning to do that, Sunny hesitated with her response.

"I'm still working on that part," Sunny revealed. "My dad has worked so hard to take care of me and mom. He's always tired when he comes home from working long hours but we never have any money to do anything fun or to buy nice things. That's why I took those pants. I just wanted to have something nice like the other kids."

"Sunny, you have been working very hard at the shelter," Camille complimented. "The Director asked me if you would consider staying on after your two months are up. They really need the help. I've been watching you and it looks like you enjoy being down there. This community service doesn't bother you anymore, does it?"

"No," she admitted. "At least it's a place to go. When I feel like my life sucks I think of the people at the shelter. Compared to them, I don't have it so bad. At least I have a place to live and food to eat."

"That's quite a mature attitude for a sixteen year old," Camille acknowledged. "How would you feel about continuing to help out at the shelter on Saturday mornings and then coming to work for me in the afternoon? One of my girls just quit and I can use the help. I will pay you the going rate but you will be expected to work for your money. This would be a real job. Are you interested? One final thing, when you've completed your two months of community service you will own the pair of jeans you were trying to steal from my store. I think it's only fair that you should keep them since you worked so hard to make amends."

"Absolutely!" she exclaimed. "But I have to get my parents' permission first."

"I've already spoken with them," Camille advised. "They will allow it as long as your schoolwork doesn't suffer. So I guess we have a deal?"

"We have a deal," agreed Sunny.

For the next two years, Sunny worked every weekend at the store. Camille was a wonderful boss. Whenever merchandise came in that was slightly defective, rather than send it back to the manufacturer she gave it to Sunny. Camille taught Sunny everything she knew about running the business. By the time Sunny was ready to graduate from high school Camille was ready to take the next step toward expansion and open a boutique in Washington, DC. She knew that Sunny wasn't planning to attend college so she asked Sunny to come work with her in Washington.

"It would be an easy commute for you and give you a chance to get out of Baltimore for awhile each day," Camille added.

◆ ◆ ◆ ◆ ◆ ◆ ◆ ◆

The train ride into the District was an easy one. Every morning Tony dropped his daughter off at the Camden Station for the Marc Train to take her into Union Station. Sunny was on the train at six-thirty to be at work by eight o'clock. It made for a very long day since she worked until five in the evening then caught the five-thirty train back to Baltimore. Her schedule allowed Tony to pick her up on his way home from work, which gave them time to bond over shared stories of each other's day. When Sunny walked through the front door it was almost seven o'clock. She was tired. After supper, Sunny was in bed by eight-thirty from sheer exhaustion. The next morning she got up and did it all over again.

This went on for three years. The winter months were more difficult with the snow and ice. Not only did the weather interfere with the train schedule, but also walking from Union Station to the store was cold and slippery. It was getting difficult for Sunny to keep the long hours and shake the bitter cold from her bones.

"Sunny," called Camille as she stared out the storefront window, "the snow is really coming down out there. Maybe you should stay in the city tonight. Why don't you come home with me?"

Sunny looked up at the gray clouds in the sky. As she realized the snow would keep falling all night, a shiver ran down her spine. She was dreading the trip home to Baltimore.

"Let me call my folks and check with them," she replied. "I'm sure they'll be fine with it. In fact, they'll love the idea of me not having to travel and them not having to worry."

"Go do that now," suggested Camille. "I'll start closing up and we'll shut down early today. I know a nice Italian restaurant only a block from my apartment where we can go for dinner."

"Oh no, please don't go to the trouble. I'll just throw something together from what you have at home," pleaded Sunny.

"Nonsense," said Camille. "One of the best things about snowy weather is going out somewhere and being with other people. Most of them secretly hope they'll get stuck wherever they decide to wait it out. Eventually the sidewalks and roads get cleared and everyone returns to life as usual. But it's fun while it lasts! Let's go enjoy the beautiful snowfall."

"Okay. Let's do it," agreed Sunny.

That night Sunny and Camille had a blast. They ate lots of food at dinner and dessert was a snowball fight on the way home from the restaurant. The highlight of the evening for Sunny was returning to Camille's place. She borrowed some sweats from Camille and settled in for the night. After getting the fireplace going Camille made hot cocoa with tiny marshmallows. They talked into the wee hours knowing the shop would be closed in the morning because the snow was still blanketing the ground outside.

Camille caught Sunny staring into her cocoa.

"What's wrong honey? Aren't you having fun?" she asked.

"Totally!" exclaimed Sunny. "It's just that I always have so much fun with you and talking to you is easier than talking to my parents. Sometimes when we talk, I pretend you are my sister Vivian. I think she would like you a lot. You know I love her and miss her all the time, right?" Sunny asked.

Camille nodded.

"Well, since you came into my life I don't feel that ache anymore," she confessed. "Do you think I'm starting to forget her?"

"Of course not," comforted Camille. "Sometimes when we're not happy we have a tendency to miss people that aren't around. When our lives are full and we're enjoying each day, it's easy to not miss those people as much. They never leave our hearts and we never forget them. Vivian would be happy that you've found a good job and you're building a future for yourself. Not every twenty-one year old can say she's an assistant manager of a high-end boutique in Washington, DC. You have worked very hard to learn everything about the business. You deserve to be happy and enjoy your life. It's been a long day and we're both exhausted. But before we turn in for the night I have a proposition for you. Don't answer me right now. Take some time to think it over."

"Enough already, tell me," craved Sunny. "What?"

"I want you to come live with me here in the city." Camille saw the shock on Sunny's face. "Now let me explain. I've been thinking about opening another shop, possibly on the West Coast, and I need to scout locations. That would require extensive travel on my part. Once I find a location I'll need to live locally, at least through the grand opening and possibly longer to get it up and running. I don't want to leave my apartment empty for long periods of time. If you come live with me you can watch over my place while I'm out of town. I know this is a big step so I need you to take the time to weigh the pros and cons like no more commuting, and talk it over with your parents. I'll be happy to talk to them, too."

"I don't know what to say," responded Sunny. "That's the nicest thing anyone has ever offered me."

"There's one small catch," added Camille. "Since I will be traveling quite a bit over the next few months, I need someone to manage the shop here in Washington."

"Okay," agreed Sunny. "Do you have anyone in mind?"

"I've already found someone," she admitted.

Camille saw Sunny's face drop ever so slightly but wanting to be supportive, Sunny quickly reverted to the optimistic team player.

"Who will be my new boss?" she asked.

"You my dear!" exclaimed Camille. "Who else is already trained and primed for this position? You are ready. Sunny Gianquinto I am promoting you to manager, whether you accept my offer to move in or not. Of course you'll have a lot more responsibility so they'll be a nice bonus and pay increase to go along with the promotion. I wouldn't be able to open a second shop if it wasn't for your loyalty and my confidence in you. Think about my offer to move in here and let me know what you decide. I want to start scouting locations as soon as possible."

Manager of one of the hottest and most celebrated high end boutiques in Washington, DC—so this is what it feels like to have your dreams come true.

♦ ♦ ♦ ♦ ♦ ♦ ♦ ♦

Tony Gianquinto may not have had much money but what he lacked in finances, he made up for with pride and family honor and tradition.

"No daughter of mine will be living on her own until she's married," barked Tony, "especially in a city like Washington. It's not safe for you to be walking those streets alone.

"Dad" began Sunny, "I wasn't asking your permission. I'm letting you know that this is what I've decided. Camille has made me a great offer. I would be Baltimore's biggest fool if I turned it down. I'll be running the shop for her on a permanent basis and since that means longer hours, it makes sense that I live at her place so I don't have to commute anymore. If you are so concerned about my safety then you'd see it is actually safer to live in the city than to commute back here late at night. I'm sorry if you don't approve but I've already accepted the offer."

Tony was not happy. He'd always believed that Sunny would live with him and Angela until she met the right someone and got married. Then it would be *his* responsibility to provide for her. He should have seen this coming the day Sunny came to him and said she wanted to work in Washington, DC.

"Look at me daddy. I've grown up. I'm a woman now," she stated.

Looking at his daughter, Tony was in awe of how beautiful she'd become. He recalled her curly blonde hair as a baby. The awkward pimple-faced little girl that he watched playing in the neighborhood had transformed before his very eyes. Standing before him now was a petite young woman just shy of five feet tall with shoulder length light brown hair and sparkling hazel eyes. The millions of freckles that once resided on her cheeks had faded to a smooth creamy complexion. With a slight tilt of her head, she sported a smirk that made him melt like putty in her hands. He was proud!

"If you do this, if you move out of our family home and into the city," began Tony.

Sunny was bracing herself for the words to come.

"If you move out of our family home and into the city you'd better be sure to call every night and come home for dinner every Sunday." Tony was not prepared to stand in the way of his daughter's happiness.

"I'll promise you two things," Sunny conceded. "I will call you several times during the week and try to make it for Sunday dinner at least once a month. Is that okay?"

"I'll take it," chimed Angela. "We want you to be happy. If this makes you happy then we support your decision."

Having those terms negotiated and settled, Sunny hugged her parents. With only a few days left before moving on Saturday she retreated to her room to pack. She was ecstatic about the opportunity.

Sunny often talked to herself out loud feigning communication with Vivian. "Phase One complete," she self-praised. "You are now the manager. Just stay cool Sunny girl, be mindful of your strategy and it will all come together just the way you planned."

CHAPTER 5

Emily Barrington

It is often hard to tell your real friends from those that only want something from you when you grow up in a well-to-do family in Texas.

The Barringtons owned a flourishing cattle ranch that produced top of the line progeny cows, calves, steer and bulls from the finest feeder and show stock the world had to offer. Jon Barrington was proud of the fortune his daddy and granddaddy before him had amassed. It was up to Jon and his sons, J.J. and Daniel, to carry on the legacy that would one day be passed on to future Barrington generations.

Emily was proud of her daddy and brothers. They put their heart and soul into working and keeping the ranch alive. As a result of their daily labors, she attended the best schools and was taught to ride by the finest instructors in Dallas, one of them being her own momma. Emily loved to put on her overalls to get down and dirty in the mud with the men. Even the ranch hands welcomed her involvement. She was like one of the guys just a little softer and much easier on the eyes.

Most young ladies raised on a cattle ranch were taught from birth that a woman's place was in the house taking care of the family not digging in the trenches with the men. Emily was grateful she didn't have to put up with those ridiculous behavioral restrictions. Her parents, Jon and Cynthia, were always supportive of their children's dreams, creativity and imagination. They believed it was the single most important ingredient to nourish their volition to be successful at whatever they chose to do in life. All Barringtons were encouraged to seek out challenges and overcome them, to never quit.

J.J. and Daniel never questioned that their place on the ranch was alongside their daddy. Working the land was not only in their blood; it was ingrained in their heart by their own preference. They considered themselves fortunate to do something they loved so much and had always respected from the time they were tykes.

Emily, on the other hand, had another dream that competed with her love for the ranch. She discovered her talent a few years shy of finishing high school when she developed a crush on Brent Barea, a handsome person of interest from another ranching family. Emily made unnecessary trips into town hoping to meet up with Brent. Often awkward attempts to flirt would find her affectionately let down. Brent was a true caballero, always reminding Emily that she was too good for him. The truth was although Brent found Emily very appealing to his manly senses, she was a couple of years shy of the acceptable age difference.

"One day you'll be breaking hearts all over Texas, Emily," he would compliment. "I wish I was younger so you could break my heart, too."

Whenever Brent saw Emily he regretted knowing she would eventually love another man and not him. This was a moral dilemma for Brent. In the heart of this sprouting adolescent lay a striking beauty soon to become a gorgeous woman, one who would turn heads all over Dallas.

"Was it wrong to offer encouragement of a 'some day'?" he pondered.

Emily understood Brent's predicament but she desperately wanted the little girl inside of her to go away and let the woman emerge. She wanted him to see that she could compete with the older girls. On her way home from town Emily would stop to reflect on her appearance in the storefront windows, imagining what she would look like in a chic wardrobe.

One night, after spending sufficient time daydreaming about Brent, Emily picked up a pad and pencil and started doodling. She soon recognized the images as sketches of clothes. They weren't half bad until she added models to them and saw what resembled a stick figure collection. Yet, after a touch-up here or bold curves there, her sketches took shape and the designs transformed into shear elegance and trendy fashions.

After several weeks of the same, Emily wanted another opinion. Her Momma was always good for constructive criticism. She would be fair and honest but encouraging.

"Momma" Emily began, "I've been working on a project for a few weeks and am ready to hear what you think."

Cynthia was quite impressed with the designs on the table before her. Who knew that Emily had a stylish eye?

"I've got to be honest, these are truly inspiring. Where'd you learn to do this?" Cynthia questioned. "They are unique and quite appealing."

"I was doodling one night and after each pass, they got a little better," she admitted. "I'd like to make some of these clothes but I don't have a sewing machine, fabric or materials. Can we go into town on Saturday for a shopping day?"

"Sure honey. If you want to make yourself a few outfits, we can do that," Cynthia agreed.

"For now that's fine. I'll make the clothes for me. But one day I want to make them for everyone!" she exuberantly divulged as she glided out of the room.

It quickly became apparent that Emily had a natural gift for fashion designing. Cynthia hoped she would apply to design schools for the fall. She put her heart and soul into each garment. With precision, she stitched each piece of fabric to the next, transforming a bunch of cutouts into hip and trendy schemes. Her work was exquisite and not one piece went unnoticed by all the girls at school.

It was effortless for Emily to pull off her transformation. She was maturing into a tall, slender and striking young woman no longer doomed to look like a ranch hand. Unwanted teenage pounds were quickly becoming toned body curves and her complexion was unblemished. Long brown hair hung loose around her face framing a pair of big brown eyes.

Even Brent was impressed with this made-over version of Emily. It appeared his little girl was growing up before his very eyes and it was increasingly harder to resist his urges.

Emily Barrington would not require much pursuing since she was already attracted to him. The act itself presented an artistic challenge of sorts for Brent. It was style-in-motion to watch him pursue a young lady.

Unfortunately their parents were aware of the allure so each of them received a presumptive warning why it would not be appropriate to take this fascination to the next level. Both Emily and Brent gave respectful heed for their parents' concern, but they were resolved not to fight their attraction anymore.

◆　◆　◆　◆　◆　◆　◆　◆

The Barea grange had many buildings for housing ranch hands. A couple of them were unoccupied due to recent employee terminations. It was the perfect place for a romantic rendezvous. No one would look for them there and it would provide sufficient privacy and atmosphere a new romance required.

The bunkhouse embodied old-fashioned charm and rustic flavor with a wood burning rock fireplace in the living room. It bid a laid back style of western décor with oversized furniture dressed in plaid, resembling a vacation lodge. Cathedral ceilings opened up to a loft in perfect harmony with ranch living. Their bedroom of choice was a safe haven for Emily and Brent with a log style queen bed covered by a western themed quilt. An inviting front porch would have been the perfect way to enjoy the sunsets but for now there would be no sitting on the porch chatting with the cowboys. They had to be discrete.

What an incredible first encounter they shared! The two were brought to new heights of nervous passion. Emily, not knowing what to expect, quivered in schoolgirl anticipation and fright for the unknown. Brent, on the other hand, was drenched in passionate sweat from sheer physical pleasure thinking "what a precious, magical moment!" Although there was nervousness and confusion at first, each came away feeling it was well worth the wait.

The release of anticipation was overwhelming. Emily fought to hide the emotion of her first-ever breaching while tears of joy streamed down her face.

"This was the most exciting experience of my life," she shared. "Exciting far beyond my wildest dreams!"

Brent pulled Emily closer and the two snuggled until she fell asleep in his arms. He was not tired; just in awe of this gorgeous, under-aged creature and hit by a wave of adoration and fear. In the eyes of the law, Brent had just violated Emily and it would not stop here. Now that he'd had this amazingly erotic pleasure he wanted more!

♦ ♦ ♦ ♦ ♦ ♦ ♦ ♦

Emily spent the next several months trying to master a balancing act. She assembled a unique portfolio that focused on the highlights and accented the tedious details of her designs while paying proper attention to Brent and their secret get-away. She even went so far as to seek help from Nicolai Darion, a local fashion designer and proprietor of the trendiest boutique in Dallas, *Amitiés*. Nicolai offered "all the best" of the fashion world so it was only befitting that this was the name of his boutique.

"Très bien, my dear," Nicolai complimented. "You are quite the talented young lady, yes? So fresh and crisp! I would like to see more of your designs. Will you show me?"

Emily was overwhelmingly beside herself with appreciation. She always believed she was good but it was so far out there to think a well-known and successful designer like Nicolai would be interested in her portfolio.

"I will show you," she agreed. "I will come back tomorrow and show you everything I have. Thank you so much."

For several weeks Emily and Nicolai spent hours reviewing her portfolio: which designs to leave in, which ones to take out and which ones needed just a little more fine tuning. Many days their sessions got away from them and hours passed in the blink of an eye. Emily started volunteering at the boutique to pick Nicolai's brain.

It was a slow afternoon. While covering the shop for Nicolai who was out running errands, Emily found herself browsing through papers lying around the office. She didn't mean to pry but something familiar caught her eye and curiosity got the best of her. Sitting on the corner of Nicolai's desk was one of Emily's designs that he had suggested she remove from her portfolio. She couldn't imagine why he would still have it at the shop.

"This has already been done. You want originals only," he had insisted.

Emily picked up the sketch from the desk and accidentally knocked the other papers to the floor. As she bent to pick them up she noticed a letter referring to the "enclosed design." The design being referred to was the one in her hand—her design that Nicolai had suggested she discard. She continued reading the letter informing Nicolai that his design had been selected for a spotlight article in the next edition of *Haute Craze*, a couture magazine based in San Francisco. The letter went on to suggest that Nicolai would be very well compensated for the article and use of his design.

"Oh my," she gasped.

Her head was spinning from confusion. She trusted Nicolai. How could he betray her and claim one of her designs as his own? She quickly gathered up the papers that had fallen to the floor and replaced them atop the desk.

"He will never get away with this," she vowed.

Before leaving the store she made a copy of the letter, as well as her design, leaving Nicolai's copy in the office. She did not want Nicolai to know that she was on to him. She quickly wrote him a note apologizing for having to leave before he returned.

"I have a prior commitment that slipped my mind. Please forgive me," she added. It was best to keep him believing that all was well.

As Emily hurried home to tell her parents, it occurred to her that she no longer had the original sketch of the design. After Nicolai went through each one he set aside those to be discarded and it never occurred to Emily to take them with her. He must have submitted her original to the magazine.

"Not to worry. Daddy will help me figure this out," she reassured herself.

◆ ◆ ◆ ◆ ◆ ◆ ◆ ◆

Jon Barrington never claimed to know anything about fashion but he did know plenty about his daughter. Emily was not one to keep secrets from her parents or so he believed. Based on that belief he knew Emily was telling the truth about Nicolai. Unfortunately, without the original sketch to prove it was her design there was no forcing him to come clean. Since there is more than one way to skin a cat Jon simply put some of his cattle ranching money to good use and, unbeknownst to Emily, he bought *Haute Craze*. Knowing absolutely nothing about running a fashion magazine, Jon hired the best in the business to run it for him swearing them to secrecy about his anonymity as owner.

He tried for months to get someone at *Haute Craze* to provide him with an explanation as to why the article was killed, but the only answer Nicolai could get was that the magazine changed the layout for the next edition and the piece on his design was no longer a good fit. Nicolai was beside himself with embarrassment; he told everyone about the upcoming article. Having quietly struggled over the last few years to create successful designs, this article had the potential to turn things around for him. *Amitiés* was in the red and it was Nicolai's last chance to save his career. When *Amitiés* closed its doors, Jon Barrington was quite pleased with himself.

"Well that's the best news I've heard all day," Cynthia exclaimed. "It seems you have your vindication Emily. I don't think Mr. Darion will be causing you any more grief. Can we all get back to the business at hand now?"

"That's so weird," replied Emily. "I spent a lot of time at *Amitiés* and had no idea the shop was failing."

"So what happens now?" inquired Cynthia. "You put off making a decision about school for far too long. Can we discuss what university you're planning to attend in the fall?"

As Cynthia was finishing her sentence, Jon was hanging up from a phone call. He didn't look happy.

"Before we move on to college I'd like to discuss something else," he interjected. Directing his focus toward Emily, he continued. "Last week I heard some ugly gossip about you and Brent Barea. It seems a nasty rumor is spreading that you and he were seen coming out of a bunkhouse on the Barea ranch. Of course I quickly defended your reputation and firmly stated that you were aware it was inappropriate to do such a thing because your mother and I had already spoken to you about it. This phone call just confirmed the rumor. Is there anything you'd like to say Emily?"

Emily knew she was caught. Deceiving her parents was one thing; what they didn't know wasn't hurting them. But she wouldn't outright lie to them about it now. The secret was out and she was relieved. Brent was too obsessed with her now and she wasn't comfortable with their affair anymore.

♦ ♦ ♦ ♦ ♦ ♦ ♦ ♦

Patience was usually one of Brent's more admirable qualities. Emily would be eighteen this year but until then, it was still improper for her to be dating a twenty-two year old man. Consequently, it was necessary to keep sneaking around for a few more months. Brent's tolerance was running thin.

He doted on Emily every chance he got but the frequency of their trysts was diminishing and he had to compete for Emily's attention even though she no longer worked at *Amitiés*. Between her love for designing and her family duties there was precious little time left for him. Life was always a gift to Brent so when it introduced him to a few bumps along the way he was not usually deterred. However, it agitated him now that Emily's lack of time for him was getting under his skin.

"Why can't I just go about my responsibilities and focus on my tasks at hand?" Brent questioned himself aloud. "This darlin's got me all tied up in knots." With that, he motioned a quick shudder. "Shake it off, Brent boy. You've got work to do."

Brent got up off the ground glancing around to be sure no one heard him. Not a soul in sight so he shook the cobwebs from his head and climbed up on his horse. After a quick stroke of his mane and a friendly "giddy-up", Brent and Brazen were on their way across the grange.

"Come on boy. How 'bout we go comb out those tangles, brush the mud off your legs and get you settled in for the night?" Brent suggested to Brazen. "It's been a long day and I could use a cold beer."

Half a mile out from the stables Brent got off Brazen and walked him the rest of the way. His pulse and respiration were racy and Brent wanted to ensure Brazen cooled down before settling in for the night. Once the saddle was removed and the sweat and dirt were wiped clean from the bridle, Brent began his routine of helping Brazen strengthen his back. He placed his fingers just behind the girth area and pressed upwards. Brazen arched his back slightly and they both repeated the motions a few more times. Finally, Brent brushed Brazen's hair flat and checked his hooves for any rocks he might have picked up along the way.

As Brent was leading Brazen into his stall, he heard the creaking of the front door.

"I'm down here," he called out.

Sticking his head out from Brazen's stall, Brent was surprised to see Jon Barrington approaching.

"Mr. Barrington, you startled me!" exclaimed Brent. "What brings you out here tonight?"

"Emily," Jon responded curtly. "It seems you didn't heed the warnings your daddy gave you awhile back about getting involved with my daughter. I'm not here for any explanation about why you went against our wishes but I do want your word that it's over. You find a way to let Emily down easy now and this matter goes away."

"And if I don't agree?" queried Brent.

"Then we can let the sheriff explain to you what the consequences are for statutory rape," Jon threatened.

"Mr. Barrington, I . . ." was all Brent could get out of his mouth before the room went black. He never saw the punch coming. When he came around, the sheriff was kneeling over him softly slapping his cheek. Three deputies were standing next to Jon Barrington and Clinton Barea, Brent's dad.

"Are you okay?" asked the sheriff.

Before he could answer Jon Barrington added, "You left me no choice son. I told you how this was going to work."

"You can't prove anything without Emily and she will never go along with this farce of a charge. We love each other and she'll be eighteen in a couple of months," Brent fought back. "Why can't you just leave . . ." This time his father interrupted.

"Emily has already admitted everything to the sheriff," informed Clinton. "It looks like you're going down to the station until we can get this mess cleared up. Just keep your head about you until I get there with our lawyer."

◆　◆　◆　◆　◆　◆　◆　◆

For the next four years the Barea ranch in Wyoming became home to Brent. He would have preferred staying in Dallas but the ultimatum he was given offered moving to Wyoming or facing a stint in Hutchins State Prison. His lawyer negotiated a very good deal and at Emily's insistence Jon Barrington agreed to the terms. Since Emily was a minor during the affair, Jon Barrington held all the power over where Brent would spend the next few years. It was not Jon's intention to ruin his life, he just wanted Brent out of Dallas immediately to ensure Emily's chance of moving on with no interference from him.

The news made it to Wyoming that Emily had graduated from high school and attended the Art Institute for her degree in fashion. She excelled during college, completed her studies with honors and was slated to finish a semester early in December. Brent was planning to return to Dallas in the spring after his four-year exile concluded. He believed they would pick up their romance where it had paused and now that Emily was twenty-one Jon Barrington had no power to stop them.

Shortly after the Christmas holiday, while talking with his daddy about his plans to return to Dallas, Brent heard the news that would shatter his dreams. Emily entered and won a contest in *Haute Craze* magazine, selecting her designs to be presented under her own label at Fashion Week in New York City. Emily was leaving in February for the event and the last Clinton Barea heard she was planning to remain in New York to launch her career.

Brent knew he could never fit into a life in New York City. Ranching was in his blood. It was who he was and what he did, and it was probably where he'd die.

Emily was being taken away from Brent forever and the timing was just too perfect. Something about this contest bothered him.

CHAPTER 6

Antonia Liora Courtlandt

Marietta, Georgia in the center of Cobb County and situated between Atlanta to the south and the North Georgia Mountains became home to the Courtlandt family in 1972. Vincent and Aline were true Dutch Nationals from The Netherlands who came to America bringing with them a strong sense of ancestral values. Their appreciation for family was acquired through living with and caring for their parents until each one passed much before their time. They had a stout desire to take full advantage of the opportunities America had to offer.

Leaving their homeland was difficult but it was always a dream of Vincent's to live in America. Now was the time to make the journey before they started their own family. As is the case with most young couples, both of them worked outside the home and they believed for a better future. They had long ago decided that the advantages were greater in the States. Vincent could make a better living and provide well for his family when the time came for Aline to be home with the children.

Although getting pregnant seemed like the easiest thing in the world, it wasn't for Aline. Several years had gone by since they came to settle in Georgia and she was starting to resent the years they spent caring for their ailing parents, rather than starting a family of their own. She knew for a woman over the age of thirty-five conceiving would become more difficult and infertility would increase with age. She would be thirty-five next month and the window of opportunity was closing.

Neither Aline nor Vincent was ready to give up on having children. If they couldn't make it happen naturally, adoption was always an option. They worried that their age might hinder the application process but their income far exceeded the requirements of the agency and they prayed their portfolio would outweigh their advanced maturity.

After moving to America, Vincent spent the next few years completing his studies for a master's degree in Industrial Psychology while working fulltime. Upon graduation his company promoted him to a more appropriate position. His new job responsibilities were to hire, train, and manage the company's employees, and to improve the laboring conditions and productivity of the workers. He strived to succeed and eventually made a good enough living to provide for himself, his wife and several children. Who better to help raise a child than someone educated and skilled in the art of counseling and problem solving?

Would it be enough? Would their application for adoption be accepted? Before signing with this new agency, they both agreed this would be the last time. Vincent feared his wife's reaction if they were denied this last opportunity because Aline could not take another disappointment. In order to better their chances of bringing a child into their family, Aline quit her job. If they were not blessed with a family now, it wasn't meant to be. After many years of discontent and rejection it was all coming down to this moment!

◆ ◆ ◆ ◆ ◆ ◆ ◆ ◆

"The baby was born with a medical condition known as ASD," the social worker explained to Vincent and Aline. "Atrial Septal Defect is a hole in the septum between the heart's upper two chambers. This hole allows the blood to pass from the left side of her heart to the right side."

Vincent and Aline were ecstatic that the agency was considering them as adoptive parents for this baby, but they wanted all the facts before making a final decision.

"What exactly does that mean?" inquired Aline. "Does she have a chance to beat this or not?"

"It means that the oxygen-rich blood might mix with oxygen-poor blood and can cause the oxygen-rich blood to pump into the lungs a second time."

"Miss Adams," interrupted Vincent, "is this condition permanent or can the baby recover?"

"With the proper medical treatment the doctors believe she can make a full recovery in a few years. Over the past twenty years or so great strides have been made in this field. As a result, she can grow to be an adult and live a normal, active life. Unfortunately for her, the medical treatment is costly. There are very few couples that are willing to adopt a baby with a heart defect. In fact, you're the only couple I'm aware of who is even considering it. Eventually her defect will have to be repaired if it does not close on its own," Miss Adams added.

"I want to make sure I understand you," stated Aline. "This child that we are eligible to adopt has a birth defect that can be reversed by either time or medical treatment. Is that correct?"

"That is correct," assured Miss Adams. "She will need to be watched closely and be under a doctor's care until the hole either closes on its own or the doctor determines that surgery is necessary to close it up."

"Why is the birth mother giving her up?" asked Vincent.

"Because she can't provide the medical care her daughter needs and she wants her to have every possible chance at a good life," answered Miss Adams.

◆ ◆ ◆ ◆ ◆ ◆ ◆ ◆

Antonia came to her new family just three days before Thanksgiving. She was a precious little girl with big blue eyes and blonde curly locks, only two months old. As she was truly a gift from God, she came to be called by her middle name Liora, meaning "God's gift of light to me." As far as Aline and Vincent were concerned there was no brighter light in the Courtlandt home than their new baby girl. It was a blessing and a miracle to have Liora in the family. Since they were so grateful for a chance to be parents, it was only appropriate that she arrived in time for Thanksgiving Day!

Each year the Courtlandt family had more to be grateful for during the holiday season. Independently Liora was a strong little lady. However, the hole in her heart was not closing on its own so her doctor was recommending surgery at age four. It would give her time to recover and gain her strength before starting school. She was a petite child and the doctor would have preferred the Courtlandts hold Liora back for another year, but she was so bright and full of life and curiosity that they didn't want this to stand in her way of developing with the same natural progression as her peers. They would proceed with the surgery right after the New Year.

The surgery was very long. After waiting and worrying, Liora came through the operation with flying colors.

"It will be a long recovery period for her," explained the surgeon. "She'll need time to recuperate from the surgery itself and then we'll start with therapy. I estimate in four to six months she'll be fully recovered physically. I would also suggest some counseling to make sure she adjusts emotionally to all the stress attached to a situation like this one. I know a wonderful child psychologist who would be a good fit for Liora."

"Doc," replied Vincent, "I'm a psychologist so that won't be necessary."

"Mr. Courtlandt, I have no doubt you are a wonderful psychologist but I think Liora needs someone who specializes in children. As a professional, I'm sure you understand that we should never treat our own family members," pleaded the doctor. "I urge you to let her see my colleague. It would be better for everyone, especially Liora."

"Alright, I won't argue," conceded Vincent. "Do you think as long as there are no complications Liora will be able to run and jump as every other five year old by the time school starts?"

"Absolutely!" assured the doctor. "Now go see your daughter. She'll sleep for several hours but it's good for her to sense you both there and to see you when she wakes up."

The next several months were stressful for Aline. Although Liora's recovery was going smoothly, she couldn't help worrying about everything, every little movement. She became so obsessed that the cardiac surgeon suggested Aline also speak with a counselor because her constant worrying was smothering Liora. Vincent knew

Aline would be okay in time but he agreed with the doctor. They just loved this little girl so much that to lose her would mean losing themselves.

◆ ◆ ◆ ◆ ◆ ◆ ◆ ◆

The first day of school was full of excitement. While Liora was insisting she wanted to wear the orange outfit with the squirrels, Aline kept insisting she would feel much better in the blue dress.

"Let her wear what she wants honey," urged Vincent. "She's only starting kindergarten. If you fight her every step of the way you'll be exhausted by the time she graduates from high school. Save your strength and remember from the old country 'live and let live' okay?"

"I just can't believe how normal she seems all the time," added Aline.

"Of course she's normal. Why would you say such a thing?" questioned Vincent.

"That didn't come out right," corrected Aline. "What I meant was she has so much life and energy, you would never know she just had heart surgery nine months ago. I'm afraid she might not be fully recovered and all this excitement will be too much for her heart."

"The doctor said she's completely recovered and there are no restrictions on what she can do. You have to stop worrying and just enjoy her," reassured Vincent.

"I know. I know," agreed Aline.

As Liora advanced in school, Aline became increasingly uncomfortable at the thought of her participating in sports. Instead, she encouraged her to try out for local beauty pageants, as there was no doubt Antonia Liora Courtlandt was pretty enough to win.

At the age of nine Liora entered and won the Little Miss North Georgia State Fair, a local beauty pageant produced by the Miss Cobb County Scholarship Pageant. The Pageant took place over the summer months to kick off the first day of the county fair. Liora loved the attention she got from winning so much that it took no more coaxing from Aline for her to continue. Each year Liora entered the pageant for the county fair hoping that one day she would become a famous model. Everyone told her she was pretty enough but would her petite size keep her from living the dream?

Unfortunately, she didn't fair as well in the next few competitions but Liora didn't let that get her down. Each loss made her more determined to win the next year. Upon entering adolescence she won back-to-back competitions for Pre-Teen Miss North Georgia State Fair at twelve and Junior Miss North Georgia State Fair at thirteen. Both she and her mom were disappointed that the pageant competitions weren't presenting more modeling opportunities. On the positive side, she was earning scholarship money for college.

"Don't set your sights on modeling," Vincent warned. "You need to earn a college degree and get a respectable job, like a teacher."

Liora considered teaching an honorable profession. She had several teachers who influenced her thoughts as she moved into high school. It was something she would definitely look into as a career choice.

The first two years of high school proved challenging for Liora as she aimed to successfully juggle small modeling assignments with her heavy course load. Although she managed her time well and excelled at both, it was obvious the modeling career was not taking off as well as she had hoped. She could no longer afford a split focus and had to concentrate on getting good grades for college. She dedicated the next two years to studying and enjoying the benefits of her senior year. All of her hard work paid off when she learned she was graduating Valedictorian of her class.

While going through the adoption process, Aline and Vincent agreed to keep the truth of Liora's biology unspoken. Liora never had any reason to suspect the unfamiliar. As an adoptee, she had an amazing resemblance to both Aline and Vincent. When she was studying or in deep thought Liora had the same quirky facial expression as Vincent. And when she smiled, Vincent's heart would melt at the youthful version of Aline.

Vincent and Aline were proud of Liora as they watched her ascend the stage with the grace and beauty she possessed. Although Liora was petite in height and fell short of five feet tall, she never let that stop her from excelling in life. Her natural curly blonde hair was pulled back off her face, accenting the pale blue of her eyes. Her fair complexion flowed to a narrow chin with a strong jaw line. Full, pouty lips rounded out her near-perfect facial features.

Her commencement speech to her peers was about thanks and appreciation for having shared her high school experience with all of them, and looking toward a bright future. She continued with acknowledging how the years owned mistakes that would forever remain a part of life but being afraid to fail meant preventing any chance of success. Finally she announced that in honor of her parents and teachers who influenced her decisions along the way, and who pushed her to succeed and never give up, making a lasting impression, she was going to be a teacher.

"If I can instill in just one child the same belief and sense of belonging that you all instilled in me, if I can have the opportunity to make a difference in at least one person's life, I will be in great company," Liora went on. "Thank you for being my guides."

That summer Liora entered one last pageant competition before going off to college. Miss North Georgia State Fair, the division for young women ages eighteen to twenty-four, was the highest division she could enter in the State Fair competitions. Although Liora had already won in three of the seven divisions, she wondered if she had the stuff to go all the way. As always, the senior-most division was being judged based on beauty, poise and personality. As an added bonus, the judges in this division were also associated with the Miss America Pageant.

It came down to the final three contestants and Liora was among them. She listened as Steffie Montgomery explained to another contestant that she needed the prize money to pay for her first year of college.

Liora reflected on the many blessings in her life. Her parents were financially secure and she never wanted for anything. She had just graduated Valedictorian of her class, received a full scholarship from North Georgia College & State University, plus she had quite a bit of money saved up from her pageant winnings and modeling assignments.

While everyone watched in amazement, Liora descended the steps behind the stage whispering just loud enough for the finalists to hear, "Enjoy college Steffie." She walked away without looking back wondering "will my presence ever grace a runway?"

◆　◆　◆　◆　◆　◆　◆　◆

North Georgia College & State University offered three Bachelor of Science degree programs. Liora chose the major in Middle Grades Education for grades 4-8. Being such a petite individual, she thought it best to stay away from secondary education where most of the students would tower over her and the kids of early childhood years were a little too impressionable for her comfort level. The challenge would be with students still open to learning and coming into their independent thinking stage. She wanted to help young people form a base for success and watch them begin the ascent to the height of their potential.

Freshman and sophomore years were pretty exciting. The coursework was as expected but the social life was fabulous. Also anticipated was Liora's popularity so she had to keep herself in check with her studies. It would have been easy to slack off on her lessons and treat the experience like a party, but her parents raised her to be more responsible.

Her course sequence consisted mostly of core classes for the first year with a history and psych class thrown into the mix. Oddly enough and contrary to high school, English was becoming one of her favorite subjects and it didn't hurt that her professor was extremely easy on the eyes. The second year proved more challenging as she was introduced to the education and teaching curriculum with a little bit of physical education and foreign language to liven things up. But as always, she excelled in each class and made it look easy in the process.

Junior and senior years were an experience Liora would never forget. Her schedule was mostly language arts, education and teaching courses. As part of the criteria for a teacher education candidate to graduate, courses comprising an internship program for middle grades education had to be completed concurrently with her remaining classes. Liora had applied for these internships in early spring of her junior year for fall enrollment. She easily satisfied the scholastic standing of a 2.75 GPA and completed all of her professional and major courses with honors.

The intern programs consisted of many hours of directed observation and supervised participation. After one day in the classroom, Liora had no doubt she made the right choice to be a teacher. The students' minds were sharp and inquisitive. There was no limit to the questions they wanted answered and the brainpower they owned to retain it all. Their eyes lit up when a difficult math problem became clear and they'd give her that "ah-ha" smile.

Once again Liora graduated at the top of her class. This time, however, she was not giving the commencement speech to her peers but rather sitting amongst them, perfectly content to enjoy the words of wisdom from the faculty and guest speakers.

It was no wonder Liora was anxious to begin working right after graduation and delay getting her advanced degree. As soon as she secured a job with the school district and was assigned a class of her own, she would pursue her Master's of Education. First things first, she would have to obtain a teaching certificate through the Professional Standards Commission.

◆ ◆ ◆ ◆ ◆ ◆ ◆ ◆

"Of all the careers you could have chosen, teaching is one of the most rewarding," the principal began. "It is a service to the community. We give back to our neighborhoods by preparing our children to make the most of their lives. We embrace a career that makes a real difference."

Although Liora agreed with the words of her new boss, Principal Dr. Linda Forrester, it was a little overwhelming. The new school year would be starting in less than two weeks and Liora was hired to teach eighth grade language arts. Today she was getting her homeroom assignment. She couldn't wait to get into the room to set it up as her own, to make it less institutionalized for the bright, shiny new adolescent faces gearing up to walk through the front doors of McGuire Middle School.

There was no hiding her enthusiasm as a newbie teacher. Linda thought it only appropriate to share with Liora some sensible advice that had been given to her when she first started teaching.

"Be strict!" Linda began. "Make sure the classroom environment stays under your control and remember you do not have to be their friend. In fact, the opposite is true. They will respect you as an authority figure and it will get better as the year progresses."

The first few months were disastrous. Liora was beginning to understand the phrase "Wait until after Thanksgiving to smile!" She thought she was mature enough to run her classes in an easy-going, fun manner. Rather than heed the principal's advice and start off strict, she found that a quarter of the students really took advantage of her. She went home at night feeling chewed up and spit out.

"Your students want to like you," Aline comforted, "and they can, but you need to set very clear limits because that's what they need and want even more."

"Adolescence is a confusing time," added Vincent. "You will find the balance you need to manage your classes and reach the students. Establish a solid, no-nonsense behavior syllabus. Outline from the beginning what the rules are and remove any confusion about the consequences when the rules are broken. Ask each student and their parents to read and sign the syllabus. Kids need guidance and limits, especially young teenagers. Be consistent."

"This is your dream, Sweetie," added Aline. "Don't let this get you down. All problems have a resolution and each one is an opportunity to grow and learn from it."

For the next several years Liora set in place and enforced the rules and guidelines suggested by her parents and Principal Forrester. Each day before the students arrived, she wrote an agenda on the blackboard. When they came into the classroom, each student knew what would be taught that day. Every morning the first item on the board was always the same: turn in the previous day's homework. When the classroom door closed, the lesson began. Liora used a daily planner and always knew what she was going to teach. There would be no more failed attempts at shooting from the hip. These changes got her organized and helped her maintain control of the environment.

Liora promised herself that in addition to the rules and guidelines she had to enforce, she would also strive to make each student feel valued. A new approach was necessary. It was time to develop a classroom community. For a few hours every day, the desks became homes. Each student was a neighbor and the first step was to get to know the neighbors by appreciating their uniqueness and cultivating mutual respect. It was time to write a story about themselves to share with the class.

In an effort to encourage enthusiasm and bring everyone together as a neighborhood, Liora participated in the assignment with the kids. She didn't care if the students knew her first name, her age or her childhood dreams. After all, it was during this time in her life when she had a very special dream. Hers might be dormant at the moment but it's important enough to share with the class, especially when they are questioning who they are and who they want to be.

The assignment was to write a composition about a dream or a personal goal and, as promised, Liora wrote one, too. She stood in front of the class and spoke of her dream to become a famous model. She included details from her experiences as a beauty pageant contestant and the modeling assignments she had when she was younger.

Liora went on to conclude, "Although I chose a career in teaching—a very rewarding career—there will always be a small part of me that wants to see that dream come true!"

♦ ♦ ♦ ♦ ♦ ♦ ♦ ♦

Jonathan Barry couldn't contain himself this early Monday morning.

"Mr. Barry," sparked Liora. "The door is closed and we are starting our lesson. You need to sit still and be quiet please."

It was not going to happen. Jonathan had a grin from ear to ear making it quite obvious he had something to share with the class. "May I please say something, Ms. Courtlandt?" he pleaded.

"If I say yes, will you then calm down?" responded Liora.

"I might but I doubt you will," Jonathan replied. "Last month when we had the assignment to write a composition about one of our dreams, you told us the story about wanting to be a model. A bunch of us felt bad that you didn't get to live your dream. So . . ." Jonathan was turning red and all the other students started laughing.

"What is going on?" asked Liora.

Grinning in the direction of his classmate, Bella Johnson, Jonathan confessed, "We entered you in a modeling contest for one of Bella's magazines."

"You did what?" shouted Liora.

"We had to write a composition about you and why you wanted to be a model. We all pitched in and wrote a story based on what you said. It started out as a joke because we actually thought you might be too old."

"Gee, thanks Jonathan," blurted Liora.

"But then some lady from this *Haute Craze* magazine called my house," he continued. "She spoke to my mom and told her what we did. She said you won!"

"Okay class. Joke over," she declared. "That's cute Jonathan."

"No, really!" he exclaimed. "My mom is out in the hall with the lady waiting for us to finish telling you. When the lady found out that you didn't know we did this she said it would be even better to surprise you at school."

Bella Johnson stood up and walked to the door. She opened it and motioned for someone in the hallway to enter. As she stepped aside, Liora saw Jonathan's mother and another woman enter the room.

"Are you kidding me?" questioned Liora in total disbelief. Her face turned bright red.

"Congratulations Ms. Courtlandt!" commended the woman that Liora did not know. "This is real. Your students entered you into a contest which *Haute Craze* was running to find a woman to be a guest model at New York City's Fashion Week."

Liora was stunned beyond belief. She couldn't find the words to say anything so she just spanned the room shaking her head and wiping the tears from her eyes.

"My name is Sheila Marmion," the woman introduced. "I will be your shadow for the next two months, especially during the week in New York. We will start with you here as you prepare for the biggest week of your life. When we arrive in New York, you'll have half a dozen photo shoots scheduled to capture the collection of a new designer, Emily Barrington. Miss Barrington won the designer side of the contest and you'll be modeling her new collection on the runway. We are highlighting both of you in the magazine. Once the festivities in New York are over, I will revisit Georgia and end with your return to the classroom. You will be the spotlight of a feature article in the April edition of *Haute Craze*. Again, Congratulations!"

As Sheila took in Liora's striking appearance, she silently applauded the magazine on their choice for contest winner.

Liora still couldn't find any words. Her mouth was open but nothing was coming out. She did, however, manage to walk across the room to Jonathan and Bella. She scooped them up in her arms, sharing a hug and some tears. Led by Aline and Vincent, teachers and students poured into the classroom from the hallway. The principal assured Liora that a substitute teacher was already lined up to cover her class.

"You have done a magnificent job with your students," praised Dr. Forrester. "We are very proud. Make sure you come back to us when you are done in New York. Now go and get ready for your big dream!"

That night Liora went home and cried ecstatic tears of joy.

CHAPTER 7

Liora was overcome with emotion when the plane began its descent into Kennedy Airport. Her beating heart was ready to spring from her chest as the night skies over New York presented an incredible view. She caught sight of the skyscrapers glistening against the night lights and evening stars, and the remnants of the last week's snowfall aligning the airport runway.

Butterflies erupted as she reflected on the previous two months and was grateful that, as promised, Sheila was her shadow. The coaching and encouragement she received in her crash course on fashion modeling made it possible for the transition from classroom to the Big Apple. The journey was long and demanding but it was truly an honor to participate in the spectacular events of the week ahead!

Liora was amazed at the stamina needed to make the strut down a runway. Comfortable shoes were the key to every model's success. If you weren't skilled to walk in heels, which she wasn't, it was best to start off slow with thin two-inch heels and work your way up to higher, less comfortable heels. She learned a few tricks of the trade for sticking the walk by scratching the soles of her shoes with scissors or putting tape on the bottom of the shoes. As her petite stature was a concern for Liora, she put extra effort into perfecting her walk in higher heels.

She spent countless hours training to stand like a supermodel. She focused on throwing her shoulders back while pushing her pelvis forward to master the proper posture. This created an illusion of leaning back, rather than hunching forward. She trained her toes to face forward forming a single line, as if walking on a balance beam. Some days she wondered if it was all worth the effort and it was at those times she remembered Sheila's words, "It's the mental requirements of this business that will make or break you. Everything else can be learned." Fortunately, her years of competing in beauty pageants allowed her to adapt more quickly to the stances and walks than someone with no training at all.

Sheila announcing they had landed and needed to deplane nudged Liora back into reality. They exited the aircraft and proceeded to baggage claim where Emily Barrington waited with a limousine to take them to the hotel.

Emily anxiously anticipated their arrival, flashing back to the life she left behind in Texas. Shortly after being notified she would be featured in *Haute Craze* magazine, Emily packed her belongings and left Texas for New York. Her original plan was to move in February but when she heard that Brent Barea was returning to Dallas, she thought it best to leave before his homecoming. No unwelcome reunion was going to spoil her elation over the good fortune this contest was awarding. This was her big break to launch the Barrington Breeze Fall Collection during the most popular fashion exposé in Bryant Park.

On a cold winter morning of the early New Year, Emily packed what she could fit in her car and headed east without a single backward glance. Her daddy promised to ship the rest of her things once she got settled and he made sure she had plenty of money to survive for as long as it took to become successful. She suspected that once her collection debuted, the hours would be longer and the work would be harder than anything she could imagine. What better place to work your butt off than the Garment District of New York City. Ergo, Emily Barrington had been calling Manhattan home for nearly two months.

Emily caught a glimpse of Sheila and sprang to her feet to extend a cheerful welcome.

"Emily so good to see you again," Sheila proclaimed as she extended her hand.

Emily reciprocated with the appropriate response, "Nice to see you, too."

Sheila gestured toward her travel companion. "Emily, this is Liora Courtlandt, your new model. Liora, I'm pleased to introduce Emily Barrington, your new designer."

"Delighted to meet you Emily," greeted Liora. "I've heard so much about you from Sheila. Your designs are gorgeous and I hope to do them justice," she praised.

"Thank you for the compliment and welcome to New York" replied Emily. "I'm pretty new to the city myself but after just a short time, I've fallen in love."

Emily glanced at Sheila offering a nod of approval. Returning her attention to Liora, she added, "You are quite striking Liora. Not as tall as I would expect for a model but that's why God created Stilettos, right? This is a premiere event for both of us and it seems we are this year's secret weapons. I think we just might charm the pants off them all!"

"Ladies," interrupted Sheila, "we have a lot of things to discuss before the cocktail party tomorrow night. *Haute Craze* has gone to great lengths to market their two contest winners. You have no idea what's in store for the two of you with the media frenzy and buyers looking for a runway preview, not to mention the models and designers all wanting their own curiosities satisfied. The welcoming ceremonies are slated to be the social event of the season and Cassie Davis has spared no expense her first time hosting this event. Let's get checked in at the hotel, meet in the lounge for a quick nightcap and then call it a day. We can start fresh in the morning."

Liora and Emily nodded in agreement. After the carousel delivered their suitcases in a timely manner, they quickly exited through the glass doors to the waiting limousine. It was only a twenty-minute drive to the Bryant Park Hotel in Manhattan, an obvious choice as the hotel was in close proximity to Bryant Park where most of the events would take place. Although Emily had her own place in the city, the magazine insisted she stay at the hotel to ensure they all had easy access to one another.

The moon roof of the limousine offered Liora a front row seat as she witnessed in amazement block after block of incredible skyscrapers. The view on the ground was different than from the air, but just as grand.

♦ ♦ ♦ ♦ ♦ ♦ ♦ ♦

Gazing down from her balcony overlooking the park, Liora felt the crispness of the morning air. Winters in New York could be bitter cold but this morning made her feel alive. From the vantage point of her hotel room, she witnessed the park filled with a sea of white tents and preparations in full swing. The show was almost ready for kick-off in acclaimed New York style. It wouldn't be long now before she would strut her stuff down the runway and the stuff of Emily Barrington.

There was a knock on the door. Liora glided across the room in true model style. "I might as well get all the practice I can," she thought to herself. Standing on the other side of the door was her future; a snowball ready to make its descent down the hill, increasing in speed as it advanced. There was no turning back now.

"Good morning Liora," Emily greeted. "Sheila is meeting us downstairs in the restaurant for a light breakfast before we head over to my studio."

"Great," said Liora. "I'm starved."

"Whoa girl," Emily interjected. "Let's put that hunger in check for a few days. We don't want any seams splitting before we've had a chance to brandish the designs, right?"

"Yes, of course. I just meant that all this excitement is giving me one hell of an appetite," she explained.

Sheila had gone downstairs ahead of the women to grab a quiet table where they could talk privately and strategize about the day's events. When Emily and Liora arrived, they were greeted by the Maitre d' who escorted them to a cozy table in the back of the restaurant where Sheila was seated. It was doubtful they would be disturbed as the restaurant was known for providing discretion to its celebrities.

"Who is that sitting with Sheila?" Liora asked Emily as they approached the table.

"I don't know. Let's find out," answered Emily.

"Oh good, here they are now," announced Sheila. "Ladies, perfect timing, let me introduce you to Sunny Gianguinto. Sunny, this is Emily Barrington and Liora Courtlandt, our spotlight designer and model."

"Ladies it's a pleasure to meet you," greeted Sunny. "Sheila has been telling me great things about you both."

They extended a hand to return the greeting then joined Sheila and Sunny at the table.

Addressing Liora and Emily, Sheila informed, "Before we get started, I've taken the liberty of ordering everyone coffee and a fruit platter. I thought it best to keep things light this morning. I hope you don't mind."

They nodded in approval.

She continued, "Sunny runs an upscale boutique in Washington, DC for Camille Sax. Awhile back I did a piece on Camille's rise to success in the fashion industry and I had the pleasure of meeting Sunny, who is also Camille's fashion merchandiser. Sunny buys for all three of Camille's boutiques: Washington DC, Beverly Hills and South Beach. She started out with Camille when she was in high school and worked her way up the ladder amassing more than 25 years in the business. Sunny has successfully learned fashion from both a buying and selling perspective, and she just shared some very interesting news with me that I think will make you both happy. Sunny, would you like to do the honors?" Sheila offered.

Sunny began, "When Camille and I learned of the contest you both won, we started brainstorming about how to jump on the bandwagon and benefit from this wonderful idea. We researched your designs Emily and found they transcend anything we've come across in the fashion business for quite some time. We expect they will generate a lot of interest this year."

Sunny turned her attention to Liora continuing, "I have to admit we were a little skeptical about how the designs would present with a petite unknown model. But after watching you carry yourself across this room, I'm less doubtful. You are striking and exude quite a bit of self-confidence and grace. That makes what I have to say a lot easier. Camille empowered me to make a judgment call once I had the opportunity to meet you in person."

"Well my curiosity is peaked!" exclaimed Emily. "Go on."

"For quite some time, Camille and I have been trying to come up with a unique marketing campaign and we've toyed with the idea of taking on a designer willing to offer us exclusive rights to her line. Our angle involves design and manufacture with acquisition only through

Camille's boutiques. The designer would retain creative license but Camille has first option to accept or decline any new merchandise. Do you see where this is going Emily?"

"I do," acknowledged Emily. "However, I am curious about the exclusivity part. Wouldn't an arrangement like this prevent me from seeing a higher profit margin? If my designs are as wonderful as you say, why would I limit myself to one buyer, rather than flood the market and increase my own personal profit?"

"First of all, no designer wants to flood the market with their creations," replied Sunny. "True success in fashion comes from having limited quantities available, thereby boosting the public's interest to acquire your designs exponentially. The swell in interest then allows the price tag to properly reflect the worth of an original Barrington garment."

Sunny continued, "As each new design premieres, Camille retains first right of refusal for one year, at which time you are free to mass manufacture them if you still want to do that. Keep in mind Emily if you flood the market with your designs, it will drive down the price and your clothes will be known as common, every day wear. That forces you to increase your productivity, thereby driving up your costs to manufacture, resulting in a decreased profit margin. Not to mention offending the socialites that paid top dollar for an original design whose value will plummet once the market is flooded. Camille believes her proposal will make us all very happy and very rich."

Liora interrupted, "You mentioned this deal would make both of us happy. I don't understand where I fit in."

"Provided this week goes off without any disasters, you will remain the primary model for Emily's designs. Our platform includes hosting a private showing each season for Emily's new merchandise. Only the best of the best in the social circles will be invited. We've approached a very connected individual to head up the planning of those events and she has already accepted our offer. Sheila has agreed to cover the first show for the magazine as a follow-up to her article on the two of you. We anticipate huge success with this idea."

"It sounds like it could be lucrative for everyone," agreed Emily. "Of course, I would need to see a contract and have my father's attorneys review it before I can commit to anything."

"Contracts, lawyers?" questioned Liora. "Is this moving a little fast for anyone else?"

Sheila jumped in, "Nothing has to be decided right now. I thought it was a good idea for Sunny to speak with the two of you before all the fanfare begins. We have several days in the Big Apple and plenty of time to think about the offer. Let's table this discussion for now and head over to Emily's studio for the day's fitting. Does that work for everyone?"

"Okay. Sure," conceded Liora.

"Yes, nothing has to be decided right this minute," echoed Sunny. "I look forward to getting to know you both better this week and we'll have plenty of opportunities to discuss this again."

"Fine with me," agreed Emily. "This week has gotten off to a fabulous start. I can't wait to see what other surprises it has in store."

With that Sheila, Emily and Liora rose from their chairs to leave.

"Emily, one last thing before you head out," added Sunny. "I was hoping to get a quick peak at some of your designs before the show tomorrow. Any chance I can have a preview?"

Emily gave Sheila a questioning glance then responded, "If you can give us a few hours to work with Liora on fittings, I can probably squeeze in some time this afternoon before we head back to the hotel to get ready for the cocktail party."

"Fabulous! Here's my number. Call me when you're finished with the fitting and I'll come right over."

♦ ♦ ♦ ♦ ♦ ♦ ♦ ♦

"Sheila you were right about the size. Other than a few nips and tucks, I think we're ready," assured Emily.

"I'm not so sure," challenged Liora. "The magnitude of what's at stake here is finally sinking in and I don't know if I can go through with this."

Liora saw the frightened look on the women's faces.

"Don't get me wrong," she corrected. "The designs are gorgeous. I'm just not sure they look right on me. I'm too short to pull this off.

I don't know who I was kidding. Wouldn't these clothes look better on a taller model?"

The women chuckled at her comment.

"The designs show exactly as they were intended," comforted Emily. "In fact, I adjusted them in accordance with your height. Whether five feet tall or six feet tall, they look great on you. Trust me, you are already pulling this off. I am very proud to have you debut this label. What do you think about 'Liora Courtlandt paving the way for The Barrington Breeze Fall Collection' as an introduction?"

"Really?" asked Liora. "Are you absolutely positive? No doubts?"

"None whatsoever," Emily reassured her. "Now let's get Sunny down here for a quick preview so we can get back to the hotel and dress for the party. By the way Liora, I have a surprise for you. Sheila, while we finish up here can you call Sunny and tell her if she wants to preview the line she needs to come right away?"

Sheila went to call Sunny and Emily disappeared through a back door. While both of the ladies were out of the room, Liora took a minute to admire this person she barely recognized in the mirror. The designs were fabulous! She had no reservation about the clothes but she was second-guessing her amateur modeling ability. She wanted to do right by everyone and knowing that careers were on the line this week was making her a huge bundle of nerves. Apart from Sheila and Emily, now Sunny and Camille were invested, and her own lifelong dream was on the line. It was a lot to carry on her small shoulders. As she stood appreciating the beautiful clothes she was wearing, Emily returned carrying an evening gown.

"I know this line is about chic fall clothes right now," began Emily, "but I designed an evening gown for you to wear to the cocktail party tonight. If it's not to your liking and you'd rather wear something else, I won't be offended."

Liora was speechless. No one had ever designed a one-of-a-kind anything for her. This was incredible!

"Oh Emily," she cried, "It is breathtaking!"

Liora gently took the gown from Emily and walked off to the dressing area. She made a magnificent entrance wearing a butter chiffon dress, layered and flowing when she glided across the room. The high neckline and keyhole front gave height to her small frame.

Cut-out shoulders offered grace and sleekness to a soft, gentle body of dark skin. It was stunning!

Sheila returned to the room gasping at the gown Liora was wearing.

"What's this?" inquired Sheila.

"Hands off, it's mine," Liora barked jokingly. "Emily designed this evening gown for me to wear tonight." She turned to Emily with tears welling up in her eyes, "I would be honored to wear it."

"I'm jealous," teased Sheila. "Where's my original Emily Barrington?"

"As a matter of fact yours is hanging in the closet right over there," directed Emily.

"No way!" screamed Sheila. "Are you serious?"

"Go look," she insisted. "I designed a gown for each of us. Unfortunately, I didn't know about Sunny at the time so I don't have one for her."

"Not to worry," Sheila assured. "Sunny has access to many fabulous evening gowns from Camille's boutiques. I'm sure she has something more than appropriate for tonight.

Sheila held the dress to her body and viewed the reflection in the floor-length mirror. What a gorgeous turquoise gown! Beneath the bolero jacket was a perfectly accented scoop neckline and wide shoulder straps. The floral embroidery and scalloped lace edge on the bodice was detailed and intricate. Emily outdid herself this time. It was a true Barrington original!

"Quick, I want to try this on before Sunny gets here," urged Sheila.

It was a perfect fit and Sheila loved how the turquoise color accentuated her blue eyes and red hair. She could hardly wait to wear it tonight.

Sunny arrived gasping for breath as the gowns were being secured in their garment bags.

"I ran the last five blocks because of a traffic jam," she gasped.

After she caught her breath and was able to focus, the show began. Emily's designs presented wonderfully. Liora's stare was always directed forward with a sultry expression that truly captured the essence of the clothes she was wearing. Print media did not do them justice. Garment after garment flowed with exquisite presence as Liora captured the true "breeze" in the Barrington Breeze Fall Collection.

The preview set them behind schedule and now with time getting away from them, they raced out the door to hail a cab. On the way out, Sunny thanked Emily for the opportunity to see the line in her own private fashion show. It reaffirmed that she must get both Emily and Liora onboard with Camille as this duo was going to bring elite fashion to women of all sizes. The world of high fashion would be set on its heels by this petite ball of fire standing beside her. They were a perfect fit and sure to be a huge success!

♦ ♦ ♦ ♦ ♦ ♦ ♦ ♦

The ambience of the ballroom was soft, mood-inspiring music playing in the background and quaint low lighting. Exquisitely dressed and well-heeled beautiful women were accents to an already glamorous affair and there was no shortage of photographers capturing each guest as they arrived. The elite designers were all expected to be in attendance: Blass, Karan, and Mackie. Also included on the guest list were journalists, buyers, celebrities and socialites. It was a lavish event with no expense spared.

As Sheila, Emily, Liora, and Sunny made their way into the reception, a petite brunette eagerly awaiting their arrival greeted them. Cassie Davis was also making her debut as this year's party planner.

"Sunny," she greeted. "It's so good to see you again."

"It's wonderful to see you," replied Sunny as she placed her hands on Cassie's shoulders and exchanged a brief peck on the cheek. "This is magnificent! You outdid yourself."

Glancing around Cassie couldn't help but be pleased with the outcome. "I appreciate the compliment," she said.

Gesturing toward the other ladies Sunny continued, "Cassie, I'd like to introduce Sheila Marmion, Emily Barrington and Liora Courtlandt."

They exchanged warm greetings and further commented on the elaborate setting.

"This is a huge night for all of us," Cassie added. "So the suspense is killing me. Have we gotten everyone onboard?" she inquired of Sunny.

"We broke the ice today and put the offer on the table. As you can imagine, it's a big decision so we decided to let these ladies have time to absorb the proposal. We agreed to discuss it later as the week progresses," she answered. "Ladies, Cassie Davis is the planner I mentioned earlier today. Cassie has already accepted Camille's offer to be the party planner for the fashion shows we'll be hosting once we sign our new designer. We weren't going to say anything until we had the full team onboard but as you can tell Cassie is pretty excited about getting our campaign off the ground. Let's enjoy tonight's festivities and witness firsthand the genius of Cassie Davis. Why don't we make our way into the reception?"

Sheila leaned in whispering to Sunny, "Judging by tonight's outcome and my first impression of this party, I think Camille made an excellent choice."

Emily admired the comfort with which everyone interacted. "Tell me, Cassie, what gave you the idea for this reception?" she asked.

"A sit down dinner is so common," began Cassie. "Seating charts are a nightmare for these events because you never know who's talking to whom or who's not speaking to someone else. Here the guests can sit or stand, depending on their preference and it makes it easier to mix and mingle. Can you think of a better way to kick off this week than with drinks, hors d'oeuvres and conversation? Ladies, I need to make my rounds so please enjoy some champagne and canapés. I'll catch up with you later."

Liora and Emily advanced around the room together making eye contact with influential guests and displaying proper body language inviting communication. It was a potpourri of fashion and style second to none. They spoke to people of interest from all facets of the business. They quickly learned the art of mingling in a crowd of this caliber. Conversations led to introductions, which led to photographs. Offers of helpful hints for women starting out in the business were easily dispensed. Sheila and Sunny lingered in the background and watched as Liora and Emily took in the glitter and attention.

Time passed swiftly and by the start of the fourth hour both Emily and Liora could stand no more. They made their way to the bar for resting their aching feet. Cassie Davis was sitting at the edge of the bar looking no worse for wear. She gestured for the women to join her.

"How do you do it?" asked Liora.

"Do what?" asked Cassie.

"I can only imagine the late nights and countless hours you must have spent putting together such an elaborate event. You come here tonight full of energy and life, mingle for hours with all of these people and look just gorgeous," praised Liora.

"In case you haven't noticed," responded Cassie, "all eyes are on you tonight. The magazine went to great lengths to market the two of you and I have to admit, for two people so new to this business, you're taking this all in stride. I've been watching you work the room. You're naturals. The fashion world is always looking for fresh players. Most of these people here tonight were hoping for one of two things: to see you fall flat on your face or rise above it all. I think the latter is the reality. Not a bad first impression."

Emily chimed in, "I think you give us too much credit Cassie. I can't speak for Liora but I've been a bundle of nerves since I walked through the door. I have to admit tonight went much smoother than I anticipated. After all, everyone in this room is here for the same reason. But tomorrow will be the true test."

"I hope I don't fall flat on my face," Liora joked.

They laughed at the thought.

"What's so funny?" asked Sheila as she joined them.

"Just releasing some nervous energy," answered Cassie. "Are you enjoying the party?"

"Very much so," Sheila admitted. "But I am exhausted and ready to call it a night. Would anyone like to join me back at the hotel for a night cap?"

Liora was the first to speak up. "That sounds perfect to me. I want to get out of these shoes and dress—no offense Emily—and into some comfortable clothes."

"Has anyone seen Sunny lately?" inquired Sheila.

Cassie pointed over her shoulder in the direction of Sunny approaching from across the room stating, "It looks like the party is winding down. Let me talk to my staff and make sure they have everything under control. After I've made the rounds one last time and expressed my thanks to the guests, I'll join you."

Sheila enlightened Sunny on the plan and the four women made their way to the exit.

Upon arrival at the hotel, Cassie found the others enjoying karaoke in the lounge and relaxing with a cocktail. Unbeknownst to the others, Liora was a big fan of karaoke. They were surprisingly impressed when she got up on stage. The applause coming from the audience was confirmation. She could actually sing.

For several hours they passed the time laughing, singing and enjoying each other's company. It was comfortable, effortless and natural. From an outsider's perspective, one would think they'd known each other for years.

The night was a complete success!

◆ ◆ ◆ ◆ ◆ ◆ ◆ ◆

The week sped passed with a whirlwind of successes. Liora was a huge hit despite her pint-size stature. Her strides were long and deliberate, commanding large steps emanating grace. Her chin was perched upward and her head held high as she glided down the runway. The roar of applause confirmed she was successfully living her dream. Sadly for Liora and Emily, it was also concluding as quickly as it commenced.

Newspapers displayed articles about the contemporary duo that came to the show as contest winners of *Haute Craze* magazine. Merchandisers flocked to Emily hoping to scoop the new fall trends of her label. With each inquiry the words of Sunny Gianquinto echoed in her head, "No designer wants to flood the market with their creations." Emily believed those words now.

Several short discussions regarding Camille's proposal took place throughout the week. So as not to clutter the focus of the main events, the conversations were kept light. One final event remained before it would all became a memory.

The Wrap Party went into the early morning hours. The five women were inseparable. The band played upbeat music of the times and everyone was out on the dance floor. The surprise of the night came when once again they heard the vocal pleasures of Liora Courtlandt. Apparently word got out that she could sing and the band members invited her to join them in their rendition of Sister Sledge's hit, *We Are Family*. All partygoers were up on their feet having a blast. The energy was exhilarating and when the song was over, Liora dedicated her performance to her new girlfriends.

As the music wound down and the lights came up, farewells were inevitable. Tears flowed and hugs were exchanged with promises of 'see you soon.'

Without forethought, Emily enticed, "Stay." Looking at the quizzical expressions on their faces, she added, "I don't mean forever. Stay a little longer and we can spend some downtime together?"

None of them had anything pressing that couldn't wait a day or two so after the pressures of the week were done, they took time to enjoy the sites of the city together. Sunny eventually convinced Emily and Liora to join the others in the boutique venture provided their lawyers approved the contracts. Each made plans to temporarily return to the lives they left behind and tie up loose ends before moving forward with their new alliance.

Liora was in communication with her parents while in New York so they were already aware of the recent developments. After faxing a copy of the contract to her father's attorney, she received unconditional support for her new career. Liora planned to return to Georgia with Sheila to wrap up the *Haute Craze* article and give her principal adequate notice for finding a suitable replacement in her classroom.

Jon Barrington had his team of attorneys review Emily's contract and after minimal negotiations, they also agreed it was a lucrative endeavor. She had no plans to return to Texas because she was already building a new life on the East Coast. As soon as Emily could pack up her studio and find a warehouse to manufacture the new line for Camille, it was off to the nation's capitol.

Since Cassie had accepted Camille's offer prior to the fashion exposé, she had already begun notifying some of her clientele in New York of her intention to move to DC. However, she was procrastinating on the most important detail: saying goodbye to Ben Stark. Without Ben, she wouldn't possess the powerful connections that brought her this opportunity. He was her champion and for that reason he would understand her decision to move on, or so she hoped. Their relationship had become more of a friendship over the last few years. As soon as she found her courage to have the conversation with him, she would take his blessing and join the others.

Sheila had a short stop to make in Georgia for the closing chapter of her article. She would not be part of Camille's alliance until they were ready for the follow-up, so it was back to San Francisco to write her feature and take on the next assignment. There was plenty of time before she needed to return to the East Coast for the group's premiere event.

These five incredible women knew their lives were about to change forever!

CHAPTER 8

Cassie waited until the last possible moment to tell Ben of her decision to go to Washington. A few weeks passed since the fashion show ended and she spent most of that time finalizing her business matters and making arrangements to move. There were several casual dinners at Ben's place but she never quite found the courage to tell him. Word was out all over the city that she had accepted another job and was leaving New York. Unfortunately for her, the word got to Ben before she did.

Arriving at Ben's penthouse for dinner, Cassie was met by a glaring stare. Her worst fears were confirmed because she took too long and someone got to him first. She expected disappointment, as change is always difficult at first. Nevertheless, she believed that in time he would understand and support her decision. Even knowing their relationship was now one of companionship, he was not supportive of her leaving him at all. He was taking Cassie's departure much harder than she expected.

Their conversation quickly turned to an altercation. They argued over how she belonged to him for making her successful and how she used him to climb the social ladder. She was shocked and completely caught off-guard by his reaction. After all these years, he meant the world to her and she always believed the same of him. Contrary to his accusations, she was extremely fond of everything they shared and appreciative of all he did to further her career. She never wanted to take him for granted.

Their affair started after being thrown together during the planning of his daughter's twenty-first birthday celebration. Recalling the night of Jenna's party when Ben made love to her in his secret room, Cassie never would have predicted the two of them would find such comfort in each other's arms. Having lost his wife to cancer when Jenna was still in grade school, Ben had no interest in ever remarrying. Cassie was the perfect solution to his social dilemma and insatiable appetite for sex.

In the beginning, Cassie intended to use her connection with Ben strictly for the doors he could open and mountains he could move to pave the way for her climb to the top. He seemed fine with this arrangement as long as she was on his arm for the obligatory social events of each season and offered him exclusive rights to her bed. Cassie accepted that as a small price to pay for what he was offering. But as time passed, she came to see him as much more than a means to an end.

Ben was an incredible man with a strong character and he knew how to treat a lady. He introduced her to many influential people in the city and always encouraged her to never settle for less than total success. It didn't take long for Cassie to believe in herself and the reality of her dream. Ben made sure she met the right people, attended the right functions and planned the parties for all the rich and famous of New York.

She grew to love him, not as a schoolgirl dreams of 'happily ever after' but as a love that develops out of mutual respect and admiration. In recent years, Ben's age factored into his declining more invitations than he accepted and he was finally coming to terms with the fact that Cassie was still in her prime and needed to assert her independence. They almost never went out in public anymore except for an occasional quaint dinner or rare museum event. He didn't even make it to the gala reception for fashion week. Cassie had resolved herself to the fact that their arrangement was coming to end. It never occurred to her that Ben accepted her appetite for independence as long as it was in Manhattan.

The argument ended with Ben's proclamation that he was better off without her in his life. He demanded she leave the penthouse immediately, threatening career-ending recourse if she ever returned. With tears streaming down her face, she mouthed the words "I love you" then walked away vanishing from his world forever. She couldn't believe the painful words ringing in her ears were those of the Ben Stark she cherished.

Cassie hailed a cab outside the building and headed for the nearest bar. She was hitting the booze pretty hard and before long exhibited signs of a very intoxicated barfly. She stood to walk to the restroom. The bar started spinning and as her inebriated body was about to hit the floor, a pair of strong arms grabbed her and placed her back on the stool.

"Hey there," spoke a stranger. "It looks like someone is partying hard tonight. Sit here a minute until you regain your composure and I'll get us another round of drinks?"

"No, no," refused Cassie. "I think I've had enough, don't you?"

"How about I sit here with you for a bit, we have another drink and talk until you're steady enough to leave under your own steam?" he offered.

The bartender was aware of Cassie's heavy drinking and seemed genuinely concerned about this stranger's interest in plying her with more alcohol. He approached the two inquiring, "Are you okay Miss? Would you like me to call you a cab?"

"She's fine," injected the stranger. "I got it covered."

The bartender ignored the stranger's words, "Miss is there anything I can do to help?"

"No thanks," responded Cassie. "My new friend here will take care of me. Right friend?"

"You heard the lady," dismissed the stranger.

Cassie and her new friend sat at the bar for a few more minutes then moved to a quiet table near the back of the building. They talked for more than an hour before Cassie admitted feeling better. She offered her gratitude for his company and assistance explaining she had to go home.

"No way, babe!" he denied. "The night is young and the party is just getting started. Stay awhile longer and I'll make sure you find your way home."

She was grateful for the company and didn't want to be alone so Cassie agreed to one more hour. The movers were coming in a few days and she still had packing to do. Sporting a hangover in the morning wasn't going to fare well to that end.

She excused herself and went to the ladies' room to freshen up. The cruel reflection in the mirror showing tear-soaked eyes was a heart-wrenching reminder of the tears shed over Ben Stark. Shaking it off, Cassie quickly washed her face and ran her fingers through her hair to present some semblance of composure. A fresh coat of gloss for more luscious lips and a squeeze on the cheek gave that just-pinched glow, quickly restoring her self-confidence.

Upon returning to the table, Cassie was surprised to discover dim lighting and two men sitting with her new friend. Her stranger introduced them as buddies who stopped in for a drink.

"I got you another drink," he informed her. "The other was watered down."

"That was kind of you," she thanked, "but I've had enough for tonight. I will take a bottle of water though."

"Nonsense," refuted the stranger. "One more drink won't hurt and then we'll walk you outside and I will personally hail you a cab and send you on your way."

"Okay," she conceded, "but no more after this. Seriously. I'm moving in a few days and I need to be up early to finish packing."

The conversation centered around details of Cassie's new job in Washington. She went on about her new venture and friends while sipping her drink. She suspected it was a bad idea to have this last one but she didn't want to offend her stranger who was being so kind. When the glass was empty she stood to leave.

"This time I really must go," she insisted. "It was a pleasure meeting all of you. Thanks for the drinks."

They all stood to escort her to the door. Cassie's insistence that it wasn't necessary fell on deaf ears so she caved again, allowing them to walk her outside. After exiting the bar she felt unsteady on her feet. She swayed and stumbled right into the arms of one of the men who picked her up and carried her into the alley around the corner. Her mind was clear but she had no control over her body or speech. She was trying to scream but nothing came out. Her attempts to fight her assailants were futile. She made a fatal mistake when she trusted a stranger in the bar.

When Cassie awoke in the alley she could barely move. Sensing the excruciating soreness between her upper thighs, there was no doubt she was the victim of a sexual assault and judging from the intensity of that pain, it was repeated assaults. Grief and self-loathing erupted for allowing this to happen. She drew on the little strength she had to pull herself up but faltered, unsteady from her legs shaking beneath her beaten body. She struggled to gain balance and slowly advanced toward the street. As she emerged from the alley, passersby stopped to stare in horror. Their gasps confirmed she looked as grotesque as she felt.

One man rushed to her aid but she stopped him before he touched her.

"Please let me help you," pleaded the man. "Someone call an ambulance."

Cassie collapsed in his arms and awoke in the hospital emergency room. Once she regained composure and realized where she was, her memory quickly came back causing a reflexive impulse to run. As she dressed to leave, the doctor returned. He pleaded with her to rethink her decision and stay until the test results came back.

"What test results?" she demanded. "I didn't consent to any tests."

"In light of what happened to you, we did a sexual assault kit," he informed her. "It was necessary to preserve the evidence to put this guy behind bars. You have extensive bruises and tearing around the vaginal area, as well as lacerations to your face. It's imperative we make sure you haven't contracted any sexually transmitted diseases."

She was furious with the staff and insisted that the doctor clear her immediately to leave.

Attempting to sway her decision he added, "This was a very brutal attack Ms. Davis. You're lucky to be alive."

"How do you know my name?" she angrily asked.

"The man that helped you at the scene found a purse in the alley where you were attacked."

"Great. Well I didn't ask for anyone's help then and I don't want your help now. Give me my things. I want to go home," she implored.

Cassie would not back down from her demands to go. In spite of his repeated objections, the doctor released her against medical advice.

"You're going to hurt for quite some time," he advised. "I strongly recommend you let us get you some help. At least take this literature. There's information on people that can help you handle this ordeal."

Cassie stood by the bed raising her hand in refusal then slapped the papers from the doctor's hand spreading them across the floor. She walked out of the hospital without looking back. Two days later, Cassie Davis found her beaten and battered self on the doorstep of Sunny Gianquinto's Georgetown home, eager to put the passed week behind her and start a new life.

◆ ◆ ◆ ◆ ◆ ◆ ◆ ◆

On the heels of her success from fashion week, Emily continued to get calls from people wanting to buy her collection. She repeatedly explained her exclusive arrangement with Camille Sax. The attention was flattering and she welcomed the compliment. There were so many people impressed with her designs. Still sometimes her thoughts wandered. Maybe she was too hasty in her decision but she quickly recalled the words of Sunny Gianquinto, "No designer wants to flood the market with their creations."

One individual did not care about exclusive agreements. He called Emily at least once a day, sometimes more, representing a very successful, very rich man who wanted an hour of her time to discuss a business proposition.

"My client feels very strongly that he has an offer you won't refuse and, quite frankly, he doesn't take no for an answer," the man persisted. "He's asking for one hour of your time. If, after you've heard him out, you're still not interested then you part company and no hard feelings."

Emily reiterated, "First of all, I will refuse his offer. As I've told you repeatedly, I already signed a contract and am committed to my alliance with Camille Sax. I'm not at liberty to discuss other options with your client, let alone consider accepting any offers he might extend. Please thank him for his interest. I am truly flattered but must decline."

The two bantered back and forth playing the "dare me" game. Emily was intrigued by his determination. Her curiosity was peaked and these tiring conversations were wearing her down. If she weren't so intrigued to know who this mysterious admirer was, she would have used a firmer approach to end this exchange once and for all.

"Okay." she surrendered. "I'll meet with him for one hour but make sure he understands this is a waste of his time." Before ending their conversation, a meeting was arranged in a public and casual venue.

She arrived at the restaurant twenty minutes early. It was to her advantage to be comfortably settled in and have the upper hand before he arrived. "It's not like you can actually do anything with this guy," she kept telling herself. Regardless, she couldn't deny this flirtatious feeling.

A handsome man entering the restaurant diverted Emily's attention from her glass of wine. His presence was strong and unintentionally demanded immediate focus from everyone in the room as he earnestly spoke with the hostess. He was a man in his mid-thirties, solidly-built, and well-dressed. As he slowly shuffled towards her across the room with a strong sense of himself, she observed his thick, dark brown hair and striking green eyes, exposing a cool, smart, and intellectual aura.

She was instantly overcome with butterflies and the churning in her stomach caused her to briefly turn away to take a swig of her wine. Although her back was to the door now, she felt the approaching energy through the hairs standing up on her neck. The fluttering activity increased as she turned back and saw him standing before her.

"Miss Barrington?" he questioningly addressed. "I'm Heath Vanderbilt. May I say it's a pleasure to finally meet you?"

Emily was flabbergasted and managed, "You're the secret client?"

"I am," he responded. "I take it you've heard of me."

"Forgive me, no" she began, "I don't believe I've had the privilege. Please sit down."

The server arrived quickly to which Heath ordered a scotch, single malt straight up. It was very uncomfortable as Emily was intimidated by the mere presence of Mr. Heath Vanderbilt. Fortunately for both of them, he took the reigns and successfully put her at ease. After a few minutes of small talk, the Adonis sitting before her eased his way into the matter at hand. He made his presentation by divulging small details about his business plan to invest in Emily's label. As his delivery moved on to greater details of dollar figures and promises to take her career to heights incomparable to anything else, Emily was confused. He elaborated on the high points of his proposal knowing she was only giving him an hour to make his pitch.

"I'm dumping a lot of information on you all at once," he apologized, "but I'm not used to doing business in such a rushed manner. Sixty minutes is not enough time to negotiate business properly. Can I persuade you to have dinner with me tonight and we can discuss this further, maybe on a more informal level?"

"Well which is it, Mr. Vanderbilt?" she questioned. "Are we conducting business or getting less formal with each other?"

"We can do both," he suggested. "I know you are leaving New York in a few days so what harm is there if we have dinner?"

"I'll have dinner with you Mr. Vanderbilt," she agreed, "only because I'm curious and not because I'm seriously considering any of this. In my business if you give your word it's big. When you sign a contract with someone it's huge. If you meet with potential investors after a contract has been signed it's a career stopper; suicide."

Heath Vanderbilt was suave, attentive, sincere and gorgeous, and his plan showed he was a shrewd businessman. Unfortunately for Emily, he was also two weeks too late. She allowed him to lay all his cards on the table, however, as anticipated she rejected his offer.

The evening was enchanting and not a complete bust. She was attracted to this man and sensed it was reciprocal. Emily wanted to see more of him on a personal level but she had only one week left in New York City. Pointless then became possible when he disclosed his monthly business trips to Washington, DC. This opened the door for an excuse to see him again. Emily agreed to a dinner date before leaving the city.

As the week wore on Heath called Emily everyday. He was pressuring her to commit to dinner but her schedule was booked solid with the move and it was hard to find time. A creepy feeling was evolving at the thought of someone she just met taking such an obsessive interest in her again. While wondering if this guy was on the up-and-up, she did a little background research on Mr. Heath Vanderbilt. All accounts of this man confirmed he was who he claimed to be. He was just a man that didn't take no for an answer.

On the eve of her departure from the Big Apple, she kept her promise and met him again for dinner. They enjoyed a wonderful meal together and she was completely at ease causing all suggestion of a would-be-stalker to fade away. After dinner they retreated to his upper Westside apartment, which was more like a palace, and spent the night making love and getting lost in each other. The encounter was so magical and brought back memories of her first time with Brent Barea. She quickly shook that memory from her mind.

He lay peacefully sleeping in the bed as she sat on the window bench looking up at the stars thinking how easy it would be to get lost in this man. He was calming and while with him, all dreams were possible.

She made up her mind to take it one day at a time. No expectations, no disappointments. He might never look her up in Washington and that would be fine, too.

♦　♦　♦　♦　♦　♦　♦　♦

San Francisco was a welcoming sight for Sheila's tired eyes. Two months on the road living in hotels really took the wind out of her sails. She was exhausted and grateful to be one cab ride away from home and her own bed.

She reflected on the final leg of the journey as quite successful. While back in Georgia for a week, she got the finishing touches for her article and left Liora to close that chapter of her life and begin packing to embark on the next.

On the ride home she thought about the days ahead and how they would be just as grueling as those of the recent past. It was time to sort through her notes and write a prize-winning feature for *Haute Craze*. There was nothing more satisfying than seeing her concept come to life from a blank page on the laptop to printed words in *Haute Craze*. As always, she was anxious to put this one to bed and move on to the next assignment.

Although Sheila respected all aspects of the fashion world and loved writing about them, she secretly hoped her next assignment would present more of a challenge to shake things up a bit. Investigative reporting was a different animal altogether. She'd heard rumblings of a possible story involving knockoff handbags being produced back East. Since exposés don't come up often for a fashion writer, this article needed to be her best if she wanted to get this opportunity.

Upon exiting the taxi in front of her building she shook the cobwebs from her head, thanked the driver for his assistance and set her sights on the elevator at the rear of the lobby. After exchanging greetings with the doorman, Sheila let out a sigh of relief. She ascended to the sixth floor and crossed the threshold into her apartment where she immediately unpacked her suitcase and made a cup of chamomile tea. Once relaxed and rid of the day's travel weariness, Sheila put tips to keys. It was time for the fingers to fly.

Eddie Coachman, Editor-in-Chief of *Haute Craze*, loved the feature Sheila produced in less than a week.

"It's a little lengthy but I like it. Is all of this true or have you embellished the details?" he questioned.

She assured him that every word was true. She went on to add, "These are some incredibly strong women I spent the last few months getting to know. They never gave up on their dreams and now it's paying off for all of them. *Persistence and patience; the perfect blend in a recipe for success!* I chose that title because it's a perfect fit for the truth behind the piece. I have to admit I'm excited about going to DC to write the follow-up when production starts on Emily's new line. Meanwhile Coach, I need a new assignment."

"I gave serious consideration to your request for something more challenging," he admitted. "We received a tip about a manufacturing company in Atlanta that might be producing knockoff handbags. After seeing what you did with this assignment, I think you've earned a shot."

Sheila was grinning with enthusiasm. "Are you shittin me Coach? I appreciate that this break is once-in-a-lifetime so I won't let you down. Details, details, tell me what you know."

"Well," he began, "it seems that some knockoff handbags have been hitting the market using what appear to be genuine labels. They obviously are not genuine labels so whoever is behind this has the resources to recreate designer name labels that can't be detected by the naked eye. U.S. Customs in Atlanta seized a shipment headed for Europe. As you would expect, the shipper information was bogus and the authorities aren't making any progress and all leads have gone cold. I think we need to turn this upside down, shake things up and see what falls out."

"Thank you, thank you, thank you," she repeated. "I'm on it. I won't let you down. I'm on my way to Atlanta, I assume?"

"Yep and you'd better not let me down," he retorted. "If you do, it's back to runways and catwalks for you."

Sheila called Liora with the good news.

◆ ◆ ◆ ◆ ◆ ◆ ◆ ◆

Liora wasn't expected in DC for another two weeks so she had plenty of time to focus her attention on her new friend. She insisted on picking Sheila up from the airport and having her stay as her houseguest. Sheila graciously accepted.

Most people would find it cynical that five women who span three decades in age could experience instant chemistry with each other in such a short period of time. It didn't really matter what most people thought, Sheila knew these women were special and what they shared was real.

The coast-to-coast journey took a little over nine hours and Sheila was exhausted once again as she stepped into Liora's apartment. Boxes were stacked along the walls waiting for the movers to haul them away.

"You're not leaving for two more weeks," stated Sheila. "Why so many boxes already packed?"

"Teachers are anal about some things," she responded. "Organization is my thing. Moving is so stressful so I packed the boxes according to where things go on the other end. It helps to settle in faster."

From the look on Sheila's face, Liora could tell she was trying not to laugh. She threw her hands up in the air and they laughed until they ached. High-pitched sounds were emanating from their mouths from laughing so hard. It was great to be together again.

Sheila woke the next morning to Liora pouring coffee and inquiring about the day's plan. They quipped back and forth about Sheila renting a car. Liora insisted that since her replacement at school had already started, she had plenty of free time on her hands to help Sheila.

"It would definitely move things along to have someone with me who knows their way around town. I guess it couldn't hurt for you to tag along today," Sheila agreed. "But if this investigation turns troublesome and things heat up, I can't put your safety in jeopardy. If and when that happens, you back out. Promise?"

Liora brushed off her suggestion with the simple response, "Whatever. It's not undercover police work. You're investigating handbag knockoffs. How dangerous could that be?"

Sheila educated Liora on the world of counterfeiting, especially in the handbag industry. "Replication is common in the fashion industry and selling counterfeit handbags is a very lucrative business. Some experts believe that there are terrorist groups benefitting from the profits of these sales. In most cases, the ongoing business of a manufacturing company producing replicas will not be interrupted as long as there are obvious design changes for the goods. This prevents the likelihood of confusion for the average consumer. However, when counterfeit goods are manufactured and sold under the brand name designer label, which these are, the journalism industry as a whole is charged with keeping the knockoffs off the streets and protecting the proprietary rights of the designer by reporting these violations. We are talking about millions of dollars in sales per year. What I'm trying to stop here in Atlanta could make some people very angry and the situation could very well become dangerous."

"Wow!" exclaimed Liora. "And I thought you only wrote about things like models, designers, clothes, shoes, and that kind of stuff."

"For the most part," Sheila began, "that's exactly the content for most of my articles. But once in a blue moon something really juicy comes along and it's a dream to get a shot at cracking the story. If I can uncover anything about where these handbags are being manufactured, I can help the authorities solve their case and that would be a huge feather in my career cap. I'm not saying it will get messy but if it does, I can't put your safety at risk, okay?"

"Alright," conceded Liora. "But packing isn't all that much fun and I'm really bored. So let's go see what we can find out today and we'll cross that bridge when, or if, we come to it."

Sheila just shook her head and let it go. No use getting worked up about something that hasn't happened yet.

The two women headed out to check the warehouse where authorities believed the knockoffs were being manufactured. The police stakeouts produced no leads and without concrete evidence to support their suspicions, judges repeatedly refused search warrants. Too many man-hours had already been spent on surveillance so the case remained open but was not actively being worked. Fortunately for Sheila, she was not law enforcement and operated under a different set of rules.

The warehouse was easy to find. It was situated on Kingsboro Road in an area along the railroad tracks of the industrial-warehouse district. The building sat on several acres of land with the closest neighbor about a quarter mile down the road. From their vantage point across the street in an undeveloped lot, it didn't appear from the outside that there was activity inside. A few trucks were parked in the shipping and receiving bays but nothing was being loaded or unloaded and there was no sign of life.

Sheila took this opportunity to fill Liora in on what she knew and why it was suspected that the knockoffs were coming from this warehouse. She explained that while the warehouse was conducting a legitimate business of manufacturing and distributing children's clothes and accessories, an influx of knockoff designer handbags at the Atlanta area flea markets suggested that the goods were coming from somewhere locally. A delivery truck from this warehouse believed to have distributed knockoffs to a vendor was seen leaving one of the flea markets. When police stopped the truck and conducted a search, the vehicle was empty. They also questioned the vendor who was seen talking with the delivery driver but after checking his inventory, they turned up nothing. They don't know how the goods are being moved or where they went after the truck delivered them to the flea market. Numerous stakeouts were conducted but no evidence was ever discovered. Without the cooperation of a judge, they have no probable cause to stop any of the trucks leaving the warehouse. The investigation has been going on for months but because their hands were tied, the trail went cold. Until some new developments emerge, the authorities have nothing further to go on.

"That's when my editor, Coach, decided it wouldn't be obstructing a police investigation if he sent a reporter to check things out now since the police investigation is all but finished," Sheila explained. "And here I am with you. We've been sitting in your car for hours and obviously there's no activity so I say we go home and come back after nightfall. If the knockoffs are coming from this warehouse and whoever is responsible knows the police have backed off, they might try moving a shipment at night. I would like to make one stop before we head back to your place."

On the way home, they stopped at the Atlanta city government office to check on the business license for the warehouse. All of the paperwork seemed to be in order. Sheila had the clerk make copies of the papers so she could look at them more closely back at Liora's apartment. Using a computer set up for public access, she conducted a quick search of the Georgia Office of the Secretary of State, which also revealed that the company was in good standing.

"Let's go," she directed Liora. "There's nothing out of the ordinary here."

After spending the rest of the afternoon relaxing and catching up, they enjoyed a nice steak dinner and bottle of wine. They headed back to the warehouse for more surveillance once night fell.

As they approached the lot where they parked earlier that day, Sheila instructed Liora to turn off the headlights so they wouldn't attract attention. This time there was noticeable activity in the truck bays. A dozen men were working vigilantly to load boxes of merchandise onto a semi-trailer truck. This didn't raise any red flags for Sheila as it wasn't quite seven o'clock yet and it could very well be a legitimate shipment of children's merchandise. They watched and waited for any clue that might contradict her theory. They saw nothing. Once the truck was finished being loaded, the doors were closed and locked, and the employees retreated into the building.

Sheila was tired from her previous day's travel and needed an early night of rest to re-energize for the next day. They agreed to call it a night and try again tomorrow. When they returned home, Sheila said good night and retreated to the guest room while Liora stayed up to pack.

Almost a week went by and every day they went to the warehouse hoping to find a lead, any clue to help move the investigation along. They confirmed through witnessing daily activity that business was being conducted on the premises. Today was another uneventful stakeout. They went home vowing to return again after nightfall as they had the previous five nights. Patience was wearing thin and Sheila was determined to get a closer look at what was really going on in that warehouse at night.

When they returned that evening, rather than sit in the car across the street, Sheila decided to sneak onto the premises to see inside the warehouse.

"The security guard makes his rounds every thirty minutes so I have plenty of time to make my way to a window and peak inside," she told Liora.

"Not without me you're not," Liora defied. "You said it yourself, this could potentially turn into a dangerous situation. If someone spots you peeping through a window and I'm sitting in the car, you'll have no backup. I'm going with you to act as a lookout. While you peek inside, I'll watch for the guard."

"We talked about this already," Sheila reminded.

"Yes, and I never agreed with you," Liora interrupted. "I refuse to sit here in the car while you go off half-cocked to gather clues in the middle of the night. Either I go with you or we both stay in the car."

"Okay, okay," she surrendered. "I think you're crazy but no more loony than me. Move slowly and be extremely quiet. If I say we go, we go, got it?"

Liora nodded in response.

"No Liora. I want to hear the words. If I say we go, we go, okay?"

"Okay," she agreed.

After quietly closing the car doors and leaving them unlocked in the event of a hurried departure, they crossed the road to the warehouse property. The guard had just finished his rounds of the front of the building and turned the corner on the far side. Since no lights were visible from the front of the building, Sheila assumed any activity would be taking place in the rear. They followed the direction of the security guard and waited for him to round the back of the building. From where they stood now, they could see light emanating from the ground floor windows at the rear of the building.

The windows were approximately six feet off the ground. Sheila couldn't find anything stackable to reach high enough to see inside so Liora got down on all fours and whispered, "Climb aboard."

Sheila did as Liora suggested and stood on her back. There were a dozen men in the room, each with his back to the window. She couldn't see what was being packed into the boxes because the men were blocking her line of sight. She scanned the room looking for any suspicious activity then focused on a table at the far side of the room. A grimy film on the window made it difficult to see what was on the table. She pulled the sleeve of her sweatshirt over her hand and with a circular motion, cleared away the soot from the window. The table was empty.

"What do you see?" asked Liora anxiously.

"A bunch of guys taping up boxes but I didn't see what they put into them and an empty table in the far corner. There's nothing here either. Hold still so I can get down."

As she began her dismount, the sound of a moving conveyor belt on the other side of the room made her stop.

"What the . . . ?" she blurted. "A conveyor belt just started up on the other side of the room. Stay still. I want to see what's happening over there."

While Liora was urging her to hurry up and get down, Sheila witnessed her big break. With a sense of urgency she informed Liora, "You are not going to believe this. Handbags," she shouted. "That belt just dumped a dozen handbags on the table. I need to get inside. I need to see for myself if those are the knockoff bags. If I can get my hands on one of them, that's my evidence."

"Are you crazy?" shrieked Liora.

The words no sooner came out of her mouth than she realized how loud she said them. Sheila watched in horror as several of the men turned toward the window. She quickly ducked and jumped to the ground.

"Quiet," she implored. "Don't make a sound. I don't know if they actually saw me but we can't take any chances. Follow me."

They made their way into the woods bordering the warehouse and advanced away from the building to the neighboring business down the road. They would have to circle back to the car when they were sure no one saw them.

"Let's wait a few minutes before we go back to the car," Sheila suggested. "I don't think anyone saw us but we need to be sure."

"I didn't mean to scream," Liora apologized. "But you surprised me. What were you thinking about going inside?"

"I need to get my hands on one of those bags to prove they're manufacturing knockoffs. We've been watching them for a week now and have absolutely nothing to go on. That was my chance to get solid evidence."

"Again, I'm sorry," she reiterated. "But that's not going to happen. You need to take this information to the police now and let them handle it."

"No. Not yet," Sheila refuted. "There's nothing concrete for them to go on and we were trespassing. We need more. Come on, let's go home and figure out what to do next."

The road was dark and glancing back in the direction that they came from, Sheila saw no sign of movement at the warehouse. Slowly the women made their way back to the car staying close to the woods in the event they had to quickly hide. Once in the car, they drove off in total darkness and silence. As they turned onto the main road, each let out a sigh of relief and a howl of excitement at the events that transpired.

"My adrenaline is pumping," disclosed Liora. "That was close but oh my God, it was fantastic."

"Hold on there Clouseau," Sheila warned. "That was too close. We need to step back and revamp our strategy. Let's go home."

In the clear light of morning it all seemed a flight of fancy. Sneaking around buildings in the dark, lurking in the shadows and peering through windows, these are things Sheila read in books not actions of her everyday life. But it did happen and for the first time since she got this assignment, she had a real lead to follow. Sheila assumed that security would be on high alert and decided it was better to wait a couple of days before resuming surveillance on the warehouse. Today was Friday and the flea markets would be open all weekend.

"Let's go do a little shopping," Sheila suggested.

That weekend Sheila and Liora browsed more than one hundred vendors hoping to score a knockoff handbag. Two hundred dollars spent and a couple days of shopping left Sheila no closer to having one in her possession. After polishing off another bottle of wine while enjoying a nice Sunday dinner, she informed Liora that Monday would be the last stakeout on the warehouse. If no clues surfaced, she would have to tell Coach that the article needed to be scrapped.

Sheila was conflicted about her decision to end the surveillance after only one more night. It would be a personal failure if she didn't get the story, and it only fueled her determination to escalate the stakes to get inside the building.

Under the cover of darkness, Sheila and Liora set out one last time to make or break the story. Rather than chance the car being seen in an empty lot across the street, they settled in along the side of the road just shy of the break in the woods. The tree line offered protection from being seen by anyone at the warehouse but they still had a clear vantage point of vehicles leaving the premises. The security guard was now making rounds every ten minutes so that ruled out getting inside the building. Nothing was happening and the place appeared deserted again. She assumed her window-peeping action must have jeopardized the confidence of the counterfeiters causing them to shut down the operation and move to another location. Several hours passed with no activity. It was time to accept failure and go home.

As Liora started up the car to leave, Sheila saw a man emerge from the far side of the building. It was not the security guard. He appeared to be scouting the grounds, looking toward the road. Liora shut off the engine and they slouched in the front seat, waiting and watching. Several employees exited the building, got in their cars and drove away.

"It's just a shift change," Sheila noted. "Let's go."

Before they could pull away a small pick up truck came from behind the building. They assumed it was another employee leaving for the day, but as the truck turned onto the main road heading away from their vehicle, Sheila noticed the truck bed full of brown boxes.

"That's odd," Sheila stated. "How many people load up the back of their truck with boxes when they leave work? This might be worth taking a closer look. Follow that truck but stay back far enough that he doesn't get suspicious."

Putting the car in drive, Liora slowly fell in behind the truck. She kept a safe distance as Sheila suggested noting the red traffic light at the intersection ahead. She grew nervous assuming the driver would get spooked when he realized they were following him. Sheila assured her there was no reason for him to suspect anything out of the ordinary. They were just two women in another car on the same road.

"Just keep a safe distance so he doesn't get spooked," she said.

They followed the truck for several miles as it ascended the mountain. The winding road and steep grade presented a challenge to keep up with the truck, but Liora held her own and managed to stay paced. The higher they went in elevation, the darker the night became. The road was deserted so keeping a safe, unnoticeable distance from the truck was more important now. Through the rearview mirror, Liora noticed another vehicle approaching from behind.

"This is good," encouraged Liora. "I was worried we were starting to attract attention being the only other car on the road. I'll slow down and let this guy pass."

"No!" barked Sheila. "Keep driving at the same speed. We don't want them getting between us in case the truck turns off. We must keep him in our sights."

The words no sooner came out of Sheila's mouth than Liora, through the rearview mirror, noticed the car closing in on her rear bumper. Before she could alert Sheila, there was a jolt in the back of the car. Sheila did a quick check of what was happening and Liora stayed focused on the road. Again, the car sped up and crashed into the rear bumper. Liora held a white-knuckle grip on the steering wheel. It kept coming, ramming them over and over again. The final jolt came as they rounded a bend. Liora's hands slipped from the steering wheel and the car veered off the road and over an embankment. A crashing guardrail was the last sound they heard as they soared into total blackness.

Sheila was the first to regain consciousness. It took a few minutes for her mind to register what had happened. Once composed, she sprang into action. Sheila checked Liora to make sure she was breathing. Blood was streaming down Liora's face from a gash on her forehead and Sheila could not wake her. She stepped out onto the ledge where the car had come to rest to see how far they had fallen. Thank God for the ledge or the steep drop would have meant certain death for both of them.

Sheila climbed up the embankment to the road above. No cars in sight. She surmised that the driver of the truck must have figured out he was being followed. The second car was sent to run them off the road. They would have lain dead at the bottom of the mountain for weeks, maybe months before anyone found their bodies.

She was pulled from her thoughts by oncoming headlights. She hid behind a bush until she was sure it was neither of the vehicles from the warehouse. Realizing the approaching vehicle was an SUV, she jumped up and down in the road waving her hands.

The SUV came to a screeching halt and the driver flew out of the car.

"What the fuck is wrong with you lady?" he screamed.

"My friend," she managed to mutter as she pointed toward the crushed guardrail. "We were run off the road and she's trapped in the car. Do you have a phone? Can you call for help please?"

He could see the skid marks from where the car veered off the road and through the guardrail. He ran to his truck returning with a cell phone. It took a few tries but he got reception and called for an ambulance. He assured Sheila help was on the way and having noticed she was staggering sat her down on the side of the road instructing, "Stay here and wait for the ambulance. I'll go check on your friend."

He moved his car onto the shoulder then proceeded down the embankment to the accident site. The ambulance arrived quickly. Sheila directed the paramedics to the ledge below. Police and firefighters were the next to arrive on the scene. Everyone jumped into action securing the car from slipping further down the hillside before removing Liora safely. Once freed from the wreckage, Liora was hauled up the mountainside and placed in the ambulance. Sheila accompanied her to the hospital to also be checked by a doctor.

The doctor in the emergency room cleared Sheila of any serious injuries. Liora was not so lucky. She was taken for surgery to stop internal bleeding. On advice of the doctor and because her condition was critical, Sheila contacted Liora's parents. Thankfully Liora had explained her childhood heart condition to the women during fashion week so Sheila was able to share that information with the surgeon.

Mr. and Mrs. Courtlandt arrived in record time but Liora was already in surgery.

Upon seeing Sheila, Aline exploded into a rage. "This is your fault," she shouted. "My daughter is fighting for her life because you had to get her involved in this drama. What were you thinking pulling her into this danger?"

"I'm sorry," Sheila cried. "You have every right to be upset with me. I take full responsibility."

"Aline," spoke Vincent sharply. "That's enough. This is not the time or place."

Turning to Sheila, he apologized for his wife's outburst. "Please understand we are all feeling at the mercy of this unexpected tragedy."

"Don't apologize for me Vincent," Aline snapped. "Liora is fighting for her life and I'm terrified for her. What about her heart? What if she doesn't make it?"

To that Vincent responded, "It's not going to hurt any less by taking it out on Sheila."

Sheila reassured them, "Liora told me about her heart condition when we were in New York. The doctor is aware of it."

Although Aline's reaction was a completely normal human emotion, she was glad Sheila had the good sense to inform the doctor about Liora's medical history. She conceded that no good would come from blaming Sheila and calmed down.

The nurse suggested they retreat to the waiting room until there was news on the surgery. "I will come and get you as soon as she's in recovery," the nurse promised.

Hesitantly, they did as suggested, fearing the worst, but hoping for the best.

Hours passed before they got news on her condition. Liora was still listed as critical but she made it through surgery. Sheila was a bundle of nerves and guilt, and needed to walk off the unrelenting feeling that this was all her fault. She welcomed the chance to shake the night's events from her bones and stood to leave the waiting room.

"Where are you going?" asked Aline.

"To get us some coffee," Sheila replied, barely audible.

She exited the waiting room and calmly approached a nurse standing in the hallway asking, "May I use your phone please?"

CHAPTER 9

The early morning hours brought no change in Liora's condition. She was heavily sedated and slept through the night, looking peaceful and no worse for the ordeal she'd experienced. Barring the laceration on her forehead, she appeared to be simply asleep. Aline and Vincent stayed by her bedside through the night while Sheila, racked with guilt, tossed and turned in the waiting room.

Sheila awoke in the morning groggy and confused, trying to make sense of what happened while hoping it was all a bad dream.

"What a sight you are!" blurted a voice from the hallway.

Sheila sprang from the chair when she saw Sunny, Cassie and Emily standing in the doorway. Running to the women, she threw her arms around them all. Her chest was heaving as uncontrollable tears streamed down her face.

"I'm so sorry," she cried. "This is my fault. I should never have let her go with me. I did this to her."

"Come on Sheila," pleaded Sunny, "we all know how headstrong Liora gets. You never would have won that argument. She does what she wants and enjoys doing it, especially with you."

"No!" refuted Sheila. "You didn't see her face when the car flew off the cliff. She was terrified."

"Let's not go there," warned Sunny. "First, we'd like to see her. After that, maybe we can grab an hour to freshen up from the plane ride. You can fill us in later on what the hell you two were doing down here in the first place."

Sheila squeezed them tighter then led them down the hall to Liora's room. Emily gasped when she saw the broken rag doll lying in the bed, motionless with a gash on her forehead.

Sheila brought them up to speed on her condition.

"The accident caused trauma to the spleen with uncontrolled internal bleeding. The surgery took a few hours because the doctor couldn't perform a laparoscopy; he did the open procedure. After she wakes up, she'll need a few days in the hospital for observation and recovery. She'll be out of commission at least four weeks. She has a slight fever so he suspects an infection and believes that's why she hasn't woken up yet. They're treating it with antibiotics."

Tears were welling up in Sheila's eyes again and Sunny could see she was tormented. She squeezed Cassie's hand and motioned for Cassie to follow her into the hallway.

"Liora was not the only one in that car when it went over the cliff," she said pointing out the obvious. "Sheila needs to get some rest, something to eat and a nice hot shower. I think we should get her out of here."

Cassie agreed. They returned to Liora's bedside and suggested Aline and Vincent be given some time alone with their daughter. They agreed to split the visits into shifts with her parents taking the day shift. They would return early evening and stay through the night. Aline and Vincent promised to call if there was any change in her condition.

Liora had a two-bedroom apartment with plenty of room to accommodate everyone. They plopped down on the couch and floor from shear exhaustion: Sheila from being up in the hospital most of the night and the others from traveling to Georgia.

"I am so sorry," Sheila apologized again. "I know Liora was supposed to move to Washington in another week and now because of my stupidity, she needs a month to recover from this trauma."

Sunny responded, "We can work around her recovery period so don't beat yourself up about it anymore. There's nothing any of us can do to change what happened and you need some time to recover from this ordeal, too. Why don't you tell us what you were doing on that mountain in the first place?"

Sheila started from the beginning and filled them in on the exposé she was covering for the magazine. How unfortunate that the first break they caught in the story ended in disaster. The only good thing about this whole mess was the lead she gave to the police. They promised to reopen the investigation based on the information Sheila provided and they were optimistic this evidence might lead to a conviction. Obviously, Sheila was not going to pursue this any further on her own but since she was instrumental in obtaining the evidence, the police agreed to give her an exclusive story once arrests were made.

They talked for hours catching up on each other's lives. Emily shared her news about Heath Vanderbilt. There wasn't much to tell at this point but it had potential.

It was hard for Cassie to communicate her story of the assault in the alley. She broke down sobbing on more than one occasion trying to get through the details but eventually gained strength from their support and got through the ugly truth. Sunny was instrumental in getting her to see a professional counselor to deal with the trauma and she was making progress. When she finished her recount, she directed her attention to Sunny and nodded, gesturing it was her turn.

"I have some sad news to share with all of you," she began. "Camille Sax died yesterday morning of a heart attack. She was traveling to her boutiques to make sure they were running smoothly before launching the new campaign for the Barrington Breeze Fall Collection. I begged her not to go because her health had not been good but she insisted it would give her peace of mind to focus on the campaign."

Sunny gave the details as she knew them adding that Camille's death voided all of their contracts for the new venture. Rightfully so, Emily and Cassie had questions. Sunny assured them that once the details of Camille's estate were disclosed she was going to answer all of their questions. For now all they could do was focus on Liora. As soon as she was out of the woods and released from the hospital, they would talk more about options. She did, however, dangle a carrot that perhaps the five of them could start their own business, picking up where Camille left off. This raised a few eyebrows but no one shot it down.

Sheila reiterated that she was exhausted and needed to get some rest. The others echoed her sentiments and doubling up in each bedroom, they retired to sleep. Sheila was the first to awaken from a nightmare. She sprang from the bed screaming Liora's name. Cassie, sleeping beside her, immediately woke to calm her down. Once Sheila was settled, Cassie looked over at the nightstand noting it was four o'clock.

"We need to go relieve Aline and Vincent at the hospital," she reminded Sheila. "I'll wake the others while you take a shower."

Sheila did as Cassie directed but once in the shower, she broke down and cried, shaking uncontrollably as the steaming hot water sprayed down her back. She pleaded with God and prayed for Liora to wake up soon.

After dressing and grabbing a light dinner, they headed to the hospital. Liora's parents were standing outside her room and Vincent was comforting Aline.

"Has something happened?" asked Sheila in panic.

"No change," answered Vincent. "The doctor says her fever is down and he expects her to wake soon. Aline is exhausted. I'm taking my wife home now to rest."

"Good idea," agreed Sheila. "Get some rest. We'll be right here all night and will call you when she wakes up."

"Please do," pressed Vincent. "No matter what time it is, you call us as soon as she's awake."

Sheila nodded and embraced them both whispering, "She's tough. She'd never let a little thing like this keep her down."

Sheila, Sunny, Emily and Cassie stood in the doorway watching their friend, hoping shear will of wishing it so would make Liora open her eyes. They went to sit by her side. It was so quiet you could hear a pin drop. Each was lost in her own thoughts. Cassie was the first to break silence with a joke. Her timing was perfect and they burst into laughter. More jokes followed and for almost an hour their hearts were not nearly as heavy until a break in the laughter brought the return of a solemn reality. The mood grew somber once again because Liora was still not waking up.

Endlessly the hours dragged on from evening into night. Emily couldn't stand it anymore and took off in search of the doctor. She returned with the disappointing news that the doctor had already left the hospital for the day. Sheila, the most emotional of the group, was increasingly antsy and insisted on finding someone who could tell them something encouraging. Unfortunately the woman standing behind the nurse's station wound up on the receiving end of her anxiety.

"Someone has to know why she is not waking up," Sheila pleaded.

The nurse assured her that there was nothing more they could do for Liora. It was up to her to find the strength to wake up now.

"She will wake up, Ms. Marmion," the nurse assured. "You have to be patient. Sometimes the body decides when it's ready. The doctor on call will be making rounds in another hour. I will pass along your concerns and ask him to stop in to speak with you after he examines her. I'm afraid that's the best I can do."

Sheila apologized for her outburst, which was graciously accepted, and returned to the waiting room. It was out of their hands. They had to keep waiting. After thirty minutes more of the same, she was jumping out of her skin. She began pacing back and forth across the room but gave pause when she saw the flowers being delivered. How odd, she thought, for flowers to be delivered at this hour of the night. Outside the waiting room at the nurse's station were three huge vases of lilies. For no reason other than to make conversation in an attempt to pass time, she started talking about water lilies. The ladies concernedly glanced at each other but settled to watch Sheila's intensity and listened closely as she described the flowers' beauty.

"A colorful array of blooms that waft a subtle scent of perfume into the air," Sheila proclaimed. "Those are my favorites."

"That's so weird," remarked Sunny. "Stargazers are my favorites. I prefer the pure white to the deep pink but they both give off seductive scents."

"Did you know that the word lily means majesty, wealth, pride, innocence, and purity?" informed Emily.

"Now how do you know that?" Sunny asked.

"This is going to freak you out." she responded, "My favorite flower is the Calla Lily. They are timeless, long, sleek and beautiful. The early Romans used the Calla to mark the progression of the winter solstice. They planted them just inside the passageway to their homes, timing it so they would bloom for winter solstice. During the darkest time of the year, they brought light inside."

"Wow!" exclaimed Sheila. "I love lilies but it sounds like you really know your stuff."

"Not really," commented Emily. "Years ago I received a bouquet of calla lilies from a special someone. I was so dazzled by their beauty and essence that during a moment of boredom, I looked up the history of the flower. It was just a way to pass time."

"A special someone?" asked Sheila. "Start talking and don't leave out the smut."

"Nah, there's nothing to tell," she responded. "He was just someone that I thought I knew but it turned out I didn't know him well at all."

Sheila addressed Cassie, "I don't suppose you have an affinity for lilies, too?"

Cassie grinned from ear-to-ear. "This is a joke, right? What are the odds that something as simple as flowers would be the common bond we all share?"

She looked around at their faces staring back, waiting for her response.

"Tiger Lilies," she blurted out. "There was actually a time when I hated lilies because they reminded me of funerals. After Ben and I were together for a couple of years, he bought me this monstrous bouquet of Tiger Lilies. I didn't have the heart to send them back so I put up with them. When I came home at night, the air in my apartment was filled with their scent. It was really overwhelming but then they started to have a calming effect on me and I was enjoying it. So I did a little research of my own and learned they help suppress aggressive tendencies. Who couldn't use a little anger management, right? No doubt they are gorgeous to look at but if I get hungry, they're edible, too" she joked.

Amazed by the disclosures, Sheila remarked, "How bizarre would it be if Liora was a lily fan? Speaking of which, I'm done waiting on this doctor. Let's go check on our patient."

They entered Liora's room to find her regaining consciousness.

◆ ◆ ◆ ◆ ◆ ◆ ◆ ◆

The doctor confirmed that Liora was out of the woods, and after a short stint in the hospital for observation, she could go home. Having been assured that Liora would make a full recovery the ladies filled her in on the developments of the last twenty-four hours.

Sheila was so amazed at the coincidental fondness they all had for lilies and needed to know if Liora felt the same. As it turned out, Liora's favorite flowers were Flame Lilies. When she revealed her front-runner, the women burst into laughter leaving Liora in the dark wondering what was so funny. They pulled themselves together and explained the lily story.

Liora's laughter quickly shifted to a more serious expression. She requested the others leave her and Sheila to have a private moment.

"No problem," agreed Cassie. "Ladies, anyone up for coffee?" Without hesitation they exited the room.

"All kidding aside Sheila," she began, "we need to talk about what happened. I need to know that you are not blaming yourself for the car accident and me landing in the hospital. When I insinuated myself into your investigation you warned me that it could get dangerous but I wasn't hearing it. I was the one who insisted that you let me tag along. I was the one that blew off what you were telling me from the beginning. I have no one to blame for my condition but myself. Please tell me you're okay."

Sheila was fighting back the tears welling up in her eyes once again. "I acted extremely unprofessional. I should have insisted that you stay out of this and handled it on my own. You're lying in that bed because I wasn't strong enough to say no and it should have been me that got hurt not you."

"This is ridiculous," responded Liora. "We're both adults here. You're okay, I'm okay and the doctor says I'll make a full recovery so let's just suck it up and move on. Can you do that for me?"

Sheila reached out to Liora and gently hugged her fragile body. She agreed to put the incident behind them and offered to stay behind in Georgia to help facilitate Liora's recovery. Knowing Aline would want Liora to come home during her recovery period, Liora graciously thanked her but declined the offer.

"I need to let my mom do this one last thing for me before I move to Washington," she said. "Besides, unless you want all of this to have been for nothing, you have a story to write for the magazine."

As they were finishing up their discussion, the others returned to the room.

"Is it safe to come back in?" asked Cassie.

Sheila waived them in with a smile declaring, "We're fine."

Knowing Vincent and Aline were on their way back to the hospital, before heading out Sunny told Liora of Camille's passing and her suggestion that they all start a business together. Liora's concern was money. It was obvious to her that Emily and Sunny were financially secure. Emily's trust fund set up by her parents would provide ample financial security and since Camille never married or had children of her own, other than a small percentage of her money being left to the shelter in Baltimore, Sunny would most definitely be the beneficiary of the bulk of her estate. On the other hand, Liora, Cassie and Sheila were not as well off as the other two. What little money they had set aside was not enough to enter into a business venture of this magnitude.

Sunny assured them that it wasn't how much money each of them invested in the company that would make or break their bond. Each of them was bringing something specific to the alliance with varying perspectives of the fashion industry. She was looking to form a company that offered a full spectrum of experience and knowledge.

Sunny's plan included Emily designing the clothes and Liora continuing to model them, as they would have done under their arrangement with Camille. Cassie would coordinate the fashion events for each new season as she also previously arranged with Camille. When no events were underway, she could help Sunny run the boutique. Sheila's background was perfect to take on public relations and marketing, and Sunny would be the merchandiser while managing the boutique with Cassie.

Sunny pleaded with the women to seriously consider her proposal. Agreeing to move forward was the big step and the rest of the details were just that, details that could be worked out. By the time Liora was released from the hospital, all five women were in agreement to give it a shot.

Sheila was returning to San Francisco to write her final article on the handbags and tell Coach she was leaving the magazine. Subsequently, she would pack up her apartment and move to DC.

Liora needed time to recuperate from her surgery but agreed to hire packers now and fly up in a couple of weeks when she was strong enough to travel. She would finish her recuperation in Washington.

Sunny had already helped Cassie find a place of her own and Emily was hard at work getting the warehouse in Baltimore up and running to begin production of the Fall line.

"It's a deal then," confirmed Sunny. "Cassie, Emily and I will start brainstorming while you two take care of business here and in San Francisco and we'll meet up in Washington in two weeks. One of us can put you two up until you find a place of your own," she offered to Sheila and Liora. "We're on our way ladies."

Once Liora was discharged and safely home in the care of Aline, the others left Georgia and headed back to their respective states.

CHAPTER 10

Two weeks later and on cue, Liora was the last to arrive in DC but she did so with a heavy heart. Before leaving Georgia, Liora's father confided in her that Aline had been diagnosed with early onset of Alzheimer's disease. He insisted that she go as planned assuring he would take care of her mother.

Emily was ecstatic that Liora was going to live with her for a while. She never had a sister to confide in and was looking forward to late night chats, sharing secrets and really getting to know one another.

"Now that we're finally all in the same city," began Sunny, "I think our first course of action is to come up with a name for the boutique. I've been tossing around a few ideas."

"Actually," interrupted Liora, "it was really boring being confined to my parents' house these last two weeks so I did some groundwork on the Internet. I researched some phrases in various languages and one particular phrase I found suits all of us perfectly. It translates to 'Strong Ones' in Italian. What do you think about *Quei Forti*? It's flashy and gives us an international flare."

"Well that's one idea," responded Sunny. "I'd like to throw out another suggestion. In memory of Camille, I thought it would be nice to name the boutique after her."

"Camille's?" questioned Sheila. "I don't know. It doesn't really fit us. I realize she was your mentor and taught you everything you know about fashion, but we need something to represent the five of us. I like Liora's idea. It's suave and sophisticated. But don't get me wrong, we all respect Camille and her accomplishments. Unfortunately, her time is passed and this is our chance now. We need to build this business on our own reputations."

Directing her attention to Cassie and Emily, Sheila asked "Either of you two have any suggestions? Why don't we come up with several ideas and try them on to see what fits best? The main objective is to come up with one idea that works for us, our personalities, and our essence."

No other suggestions were forthcoming. Sunny's expression revealed her disappointment so Sheila gently touched her arm and gestured for them to retreat to another room. It was obvious that Sunny was still dealing with the void left in the wake of Camille's passing. So many life-changing events had taken place recently and it was becoming apparent to Sheila that she may not be coping well.

"I'm doing okay," assured Sunny. "Camille was an everyday part of my life and a career I wouldn't have if it weren't for her. Now that she's gone I feel it's my responsibility to keep her spirit alive. I thought naming our boutique after her was a way to do that. I didn't mean to force her name on everyone and I agree with what you said. Actually, I think Liora came up with the perfect name. We're all very strong women. When you combine that with each of our individual expertise in fashion, we just might take it international and have a huge hit on our hands. Maybe we can find another way to recognize Camille's impact on our lives that isn't so overshadowing."

"I'm sure there is something we can do to honor her," agreed Sheila. "Maybe we can pay homage at the opening. Let's talk to the others and see what they think. We're all aware that if it weren't for Camille our union might not exist. I'm sure everyone will be fine with the idea."

They rejoined the others. Since no one had other suggestions and everyone loved Liora's idea, *Quei Forti* was born. It was their first joint decision.

Once the first resolution was reached, the next few came easily. All agreed that *Quei Forti* would cater to haute couture evening gowns and apparel for celebrities and rich socialites; those that could afford a price tag reflective of the quality and uniqueness representative of Emily's designs. They acknowledged that technological advancements warranted a presence on the Internet, but agreed to have a website for informational purposes only. Although designs would be available for public viewing, no garments would be for sale on the Internet. All purchases would be made through the boutique. The goal was to have *Quei Forti* known as the boutique that provided nothing short of personal attention and haute couture advice for each and every client.

"The objective of *Quei Forti* is to create an international shopping experience," informed Sunny. "We want to create a marriage of sorts with each client so when she needs an original design for the event of the season, *Quei Forti* is the first place she turns. We want every member of our team to know what's hanging in the closet of each client that walks through our doors."

"I think that's brilliant," agreed Emily. "I think we should also target the male gender for when a gentleman comes into the boutique to buy a gift for his lady. We can provide him first-hand knowledge of her likes and dislikes. Most men are afraid to come into chic boutiques because they don't know the first thing about fashion. If we remove that fear then we make them a part of our target audience, too."

"I love it!" exclaimed Sheila. "I'll get to work on that campaign. This is great. Our first brainstorming meeting and we've already come up with a name, an approach and a new marketing campaign. I'd say that's a good start for one day. Sunny, are you sure you're okay with using Camille's old location for our new boutique?"

"I'm fine with that," assured Sunny. "Camille would be honored. There's plenty of office space above the store and it's in the perfect location. The next few weeks are going to be hectic trying to get the Barrington Breeze Fall Collection together so we need to be central to each other. Emily that reminds me, since we are going with originals only, it's probably a good idea to get working on some new designs. We all agreed that your line would be the focus of *Quei Forti*—oh that sounds so nice—but in order for us to accommodate our clients, we'll have to include some other high end designers right now until your line grows."

"Already on it," she assured. "I'm not ready to show you any finished designs but I'll have at least a dozen by the end of the month. I've also started dabbling with the Spring Collection but I'll make the additional designs for the Fall Collection my priority."

"I think we can call it a wrap for this meeting," suggested Sunny. "We all know what we need to do so let's go get 'em ladies."

"Hold it," interrupted Liora. "Where do I start?"

"Your living room couch," directed Sunny. "You're still recovering from surgery. We promised Aline and Vincent we'd take care of you so that's what we're going to do. Give yourself a few more days and then we'll schedule some fittings with Emily. We need you fully recovered for the grand opening."

"Alright," conceded Liora. "You win for now but only because I'm tired."

◆ ◆ ◆ ◆ ◆ ◆ ◆ ◆

They worked diligently to ensure a successful grand opening for *Quei Forti*. The New York Post, Washington Post and USA Today all provided headlines in their fashion section capturing the upcoming gala event in the days just prior to the opening. As part of the genius campaign engineered by Sheila, favors were called in for newspaper headlines in Atlanta, San Francisco and Dallas. Thanks to her magnificent public relations acumen, she accomplished big media recognition for what was earmarked to be the must-attend event of the year. Monumental attention was paid to the launch of a new era in the fashion world and no expense was spared for the hundreds of *Quei Forti*'s guests who were expected to be in attendance for the grand opening reception and banquet.

The celebration was launched with a black tie reception at the boutique. A pageant of chic, elegant models strategically flowed throughout the shop flaunting the portfolio of Emily's label. Already a huge success, each design was reintroduced to offer a second look at that first auspicious impression.

The Black and White Affair donned women dressing for elegance. Most graced the night in black evening gowns and simple gems calling attention to the elegance of each lady's neckline or wrist. An occasional spaghetti strap dress with slits down the back or side revealed small glimpses of well-shaped calves. Also notable were the lavish hairstyles complimenting the exquisite fashions. The traditional black tuxedo was the attire for the men who dressed in conformity with the spirit of the occasion.

Sounds of soothing jazz played in the background as guests were treated to an assortment of champagne and canapés. In addition to being a spectacular event, it was a prime connection for deepening their network both at home and abroad. The evening thus far was unrivaled for cementing existing bonds and laying the foundation for new ones.

As the cocktail hour was winding down, Sunny addressed the guests, "We promise you a fantastic evening of elegant wines, gourmet dining and splendid entertainment. When you are ready, please step outside and be carried off to the next stop on our magical journey."

Limousines lined the street awaiting the guests for transport to a formal dinner at the Four Seasons overlooking Rock Creek Park and Historic Georgetown. Its gracious setting, attentiveness to guests, impeccable service and celebrated cuisine made it *the* place for social occasions.

The Ballroom was located at the foot of a winding staircase. Entry gave way to plush comforting hues of blue and green exuding warmth and elegance amidst the flawless backdrop for *Quei Forti*'s stunning black tie affair. The walls were garnished with extravagant draperies and overhead each banquet table hung a bohemian chandelier spotlighting a grand centerpiece of three dozen lilies in a rainbow of style and color sitting atop pure white linens boasting a sea of Waterford crystal.

As the guests arrived, they were greeted with classical piano music and soft lighting throughout the room. A white-gloved staff provided a brief Hors D'oeuvre reception of lobster salad on baguette and a variety of cheeses, followed by the main course of pan fried sea bass filets and filet of pork rolled in pistachios. Finally an assortment of decadent pastries was served for dessert.

Blass, Karan, Mackie and many other fashion icons were on hand to offer words of accomplishment and encouragement to the women of *Quei Forti*. They were praised for their willingness to enterprise outside the box. As the plan was to have the evening's festivities enjoyed by all, speeches were kept to a minimum. Once the speeches were concluded, the band starting playing and the dance floor was open to all.

The party went on for hours and everyone was absolutely delighted.

With the clock approaching midnight, Liora joined the band for one final song of the evening dedicating her performance to Camille

Sax, without whom their alliance would not exist. As she neared the end of her Washington singing debut, the other women of *Quei Forti* accompanied her onstage to thank the guests for attending the grand opening. Sunny stood before the crowd giving praise to everyone that worked so hard to make the evening a complete success and while bringing down the curtain on the festivities, a reporter from the Washington Post came onstage to read them the headlines for the next day's morning paper: QUEI FORTI—ENORMOUSLY DELECTABLE AND A DAZZLING MARVEL!

Applause rang out at the sight of the headline. They were basking in their glory and as they proceeded down off the stage, Emily caught a glimpse of a familiar face exiting the ballroom. How did she not see him before now?

CHAPTER 11

The days immediately following the grand opening were hectic. Several requests were made to interview the group but most were declined. As part of the responsibility accompanying her public relations title, Sheila fielded most of the interviews to allow the others freedom to run the day-to-day operations of *Quei Forti*.

In keeping with their promise to honor Camille Sax, the first new design was labeled *Camille's Dream*. The lucky recipient of this design was Ben Stark's daughter Jenna. Although Ben was still refusing to have any contact with Cassie, she and Jenna had remained close since her move to DC and Jenna attended the opening in support of Cassie's new venture.

Much of the post-celebration pressure fell on Emily as orders for her designs were pouring in for immediate delivery. In an effort to keep up with the demand, deliveries were set for three months out but filling them still required working eighteen hours a day leaving precious little time for sleep. Since Heath was in New York three out of four weeks each month, she had no other commitments to prevent her from putting in long hours. Liora was on hand for fittings as each new design was completed. Cassie and Sunny were busy setting up the boutique and catering to the clients.

Happy Hour became part of their routine when the pressures of instant success required winding down at the end of each day. *The Gathering* became a favorite hot spot for their stress release, as it was a premiere location for sustenance and fun where Liora could enjoy her fondness for karaoke. The owner, Mickey, became a close friend to all of them. They enjoyed the same table in the back of the room each time they visited.

On one hot summer night Mickey was trying out a new band. It was time for the first set to begin but the lead singer was running late. Liora could see the crowd growing restless so she jumped up on stage and took control of the microphone till he arrived. Once she overcame her nervousness, the crowd loved her. Mickey was grateful for the save and for his gratitude guaranteed our table "reserved" indefinitely. From that night forward the ladies of *Quei Forti* became regulars at *The Gathering*.

Days turned to weeks and weeks to months. Having not been contacted by the man at the opening, Emily assumed it was a case of mistaken identity. She had to be sure so she called her father in Dallas. Jon Barrington told his daughter that Brent had moved away from Dallas six months ago. His last known whereabouts was the Barea ranch in Wyoming. He agreed that she must have been mistaken but offered to follow-up with the Barea family to be sure. The next day Emily received a call from her father telling her that Brent Barea was no longer in Wyoming. No one on the ranch knew where he had gone and his family hadn't heard from him since the departure.

"You really have nothing to worry about," he consoled. "If he does contact you or shows up in DC, give me a call and I'll take care of it."

"I can handle one ex-boyfriend Daddy," she assured. "If it was him that I saw at the party, I'm sure he just wanted to say hello and wish me well."

They talked a short while longer catching up on the family and she filled him in on the business. Once the conversation ended, Emily resolved to put the sighting behind her. As she was preparing to turn in for the night, the phone rang. Heath Vanderbilt was coming to town. She fell asleep that night dreaming of good times to come.

◆　◆　◆　◆　◆　◆　◆　◆

Heath and Emily planned their reunion to be an escape from the city. They chose to set sail on the Odyssey for a romantic dinner cruise. The evening's meal was three courses followed by a stroll around the outer deck. Stretched out before them were the Potomac

River and its scenic accompaniment of breathtaking monuments belonging to the nation's capitol. It was truly remarkable! Inside the band was warming up for dancing. Heath escorted Emily back inside and onto the dance floor where they got lost in each other's arms for hours.

She awoke the next morning reeling from total satisfaction of emotional intimacy. He brought her to heights of shear pleasure spiritually, emotionally, sexually, and physically. It was truly an erotic adventure from foreplay to orgasmic experience. Using brushes of deep relaxation while bringing about stimulation, Heath Vanderbilt was an artist at lovemaking. As each encounter with him was a marathon, their sessions lasted long enough for her to release all tension and experience the joy of multiple orgasms. It was commensurate to an earthquake with aftershocks of titillation.

The ringing of the phone on her nightstand jolted her back to reality. She glanced at the clock and quickly sprang from the bed. Her sudden movement woke Heath from a dreamy sleep.

"What's wrong Baby?" he asked.

"I had a nine o'clock fitting with Liora this morning and it's now ten fifteen. She's gonna kill me."

Emily picked up the handset to Liora teasing, "Hussy. Get your butt to work. Playtime's over."

"You're just jealous," Emily joked.

"Damn straight," she concurred. "Any plans to work today?"

"A quick shower and I'll be on my way," she assured.

She hung up, knelt down on the bed and shared a deep lunging kiss with Heath before running off to the shower.

He shouted after her, "Let's have dinner at home tonight. I have something I want to discuss with you."

"Okay," she yelled back, "But it will have to be a late one. I have a long day ahead of me."

Liora was sitting at the drafting table when Emily arrived glowing from the previous night's sexual rendezvous. She couldn't stop talking about Heath and the wonderful night they shared on the cruise and their glorious lovemaking.

Liora grew very close to Emily while living together when she first arrived in DC. She was now envious of Emily who was free to divulge the most intimidate details of her relationship with Heath as Liora yearned to discuss the new man in her life. But the timing was wrong and she had to wait to share her news.

Liora reflected on how she met Troy at a local coffee shop the morning after the grand opening. He was seated at a table just inside the doorway reading the newspaper. Hurrying to get to work she dropped her wallet onto his table causing a cup of coffee to spill in his lap. He jumped from his seat ready to berate her for the carelessness but was rendered speechless by her beauty.

Liora spoke first. "Oh no, look what I've done. I am so sorry." She was mortified at the sight of splattered coffee all over this man's pants. "I'm usually not this clumsy but I'm late for work. That's no excuse though. Let me give you my name and number and please send me the bill for the cleaning."

He stared back with no response.

She again apologized. "I really am sorry. Will you please let me pay for your cleaning and another cup of coffee?"

He broke the silence complimenting, "You have the most gorgeous eyes!"

She modestly thanked him but remained uncomfortable with his stare. Recovering from the awkward moment, he accepted her offer. She purchased another cup of coffee from the barista, gave him her business card, and apologized once again.

Extending his hand, he introduced himself. "My name is Troy Welkins. Glancing at her card in his hand he added, "It was a pleasure meeting you Liora Courtlandt."

"Likewise I'm sure," she said. She shook his hand, bid him farewell and went on her way. As she rounded the corner of the building, she sensed him watching her and shuttered at the strange encounter.

Instinct said to hang up the phone when he called the next day. However, she owed him the courtesy of following through on her offer to pay for his soiled clothes. He initiated the conversation with an apology for his behavior the previous day.

"I'm not a psychopath," he began, "but when I looked up and saw you standing in front of me, you were truly stunning. I apologize if I made you feel awkward."

"That's very kind of you to say," she thanked. "How much do I owe you for the cleaning?"

"I've got it covered but perhaps we could have drinks sometime," he suggested.

Red flags were popping up like crazy but something about this man intrigued her. It might have been the compliments he paid or perhaps her desire for some masculine attention. Regardless, she permitted him to call again and if her schedule permitted, she would join him for a drink. An hour later he was on the phone inviting her to happy hour.

Troy Welkins initially came across as cocky at the coffee shop. Nonetheless, the Troy Welkins before her now was a more demure, thoughtful man who was being careful not to lay it on too thick. The conversation remained light with some humor tossed about and Liora was having an absolutely wonderful time. Sharing an evening with someone of the opposite sex proved to soften her defenses. They arranged to have dinner the following week. That date led to another then two dates in one week. Somewhere along the way, she started to fall for this guy. The next step in the natural progression was sexual intimacy.

Liora invited Troy to an intimate romantic dinner at her place. The phone lain beside the cradle so their date wouldn't be interrupted, lights were dim and candles illuminated the apartment creating a dynamic effect. Soft romantic songs of Frank Sinatra emanated from the stereo forging a charismatic evening. The table was set with white linens, fanned cloth napkins, her favorite china and crystal, and an unscented candle floated in a small glass with rose petals strewn about the tabletop. Filet mignon was wafting from the kitchen and the enticing aroma filled the air. This night was all about making him feel that he was the only man who mattered.

"Wow!" he exclaimed. "That was a wonderful dinner. You are full of surprises."

"Wait till you see what's for dessert," she teased with a wink.

Troy sensed where the evening was headed and it was time to set the ground rules. Helping Liora clear the dishes, he followed her into the kitchen. He placed the dishes on the counter, took her hand in his and led them both to the couch.

"We have to talk," he blurted.

With fear in her eyes and no forethought, the words flew out, "Oh God no. You're married?"

"It's not what you think," he defended.

He could see the scorn in her eyes as she pulled back her hands not wanting him to touch her.

"Let me explain," he pleaded.

"Explain how you've been lying to me for weeks?" she cried. "Fine, explain," she demanded.

Troy communicated the details of his loveless marriage. He explained that divorce was imminent but since a great deal of money was at stake, it was imperative he be discrete. He added that his lawyers were working on the matter but the situation was complicated. Regrettably, a prenuptial agreement precluded any marital affairs or the injured party would receive most of the assets.

"I've worked extremely hard to amass my fortune," he continued, "and I'm not prepared to walk away from it all. If you can't live with my situation for a little while and agree to keep our relationship strictly confidential, and I mean no one can know about us, not even your friends, then it's probably better if we don't go any further."

The shock was clouding her comprehension of his words. "Let me get this straight. You're married but not happily, you're getting a divorce but it's complicated, and you want to continue our relationship but we have to keep it a secret. Did I miss anything?"

"I know how it sounds," he defended. "But it's the truth. I don't want us to stop seeing each other. I want to make passionate love to you right now but we can't until you say you understand."

The logical part of her brain was screaming run but the undeniable lust in her heart said to trust him. Their relationship just became spicy and risqué. Who were they hurting if he was already getting a divorce? The girls would understand why she had to remain silent. She wanted to taste his kiss and fall into his arms. She held his face in her hands and kissed him hard, whispering, "Make love to me Troy."

He scooped her up in his arms and carried her to the bedroom. After gently kissing, caressing and nibbling her neck, he ran a bubble bath for Liora's relaxing pleasure. Flickering candles lined the tub as she disrobed and stepped into the warm water. For a short while she was taken away from the reality of his confession. He returned with an oversized towel and gently patted every curve of her body until she was dry. He led her back to the bedroom where a trail of rose petals lined a path to the bed. Strategically placed incense, more candles and soft music enhanced the mood as he laid her down on top of the bed and began sensually kissing her neck. Slowly rolling her onto her back, he stroked every part of her body driving her senses wild. She lay stimulated from passionate foreplay while he explored her body and experimented using his tongue and hands. He laid soft kisses up and down her neck and ears, massaging them with his tongue. His touch sent chills down her spine as he whispered, "I love you."

He slowly made his way down the front of her body. Equal attention was paid to her voluptuous breasts. His tongue moved in circular unison with his thumb and forefinger around both nipples making them hard. She moaned in ecstasy. He continued to stimulate all areas of her body bringing her to climax. After the bedroom, they made love all night by the glow of the living room fireplace.

Liora wanted to share her reminiscence with Emily now but refrained.

♦ ♦ ♦ ♦ ♦ ♦ ♦ ♦

Emily was exhausted when she returned home that night. It was bittersweet to see that Heath had prepared a candlelight dinner with his own hands. She loved his enthusiasm but was unsure of her stamina to appreciate the mood. Romantic music was playing in the background and her heart was in her throat as she suspected a proposal was forthcoming. Marriage was not an option for her now with *Quei Forti* still in its infancy. Imagine her shock when Heath revealed his motivation for the evening. The conversation sounded all too familiar as he reminded her again that *Quei Forti*'s success stemmed from her artistic gift.

"Rather than receive the recognition for your hard work and creativity, you are still sharing the spotlight with four other women," he reminded.

Heath was appealing to her vanity by pointing out the long hours she'd been working while the others enjoyed their lives built on the rewards of her labor. He was once again trying to drive a wedge between her and the others by enticing her to break away and start her own business. Since she was already tired from the day's production, Emily's patience was wearing thin and a twinge of resentment was budding inside her gut.

"Cassie plans an occasional social event," he continued "to launch your new designs. When she's not planning parties, she's in the boutique dressing mannequins and taking in money from the sale of your designs. Sunny constantly pushes you to design more clothes so she can sell them and profit from the sale of your designs. Liora has a couple of fittings a week and waits to collect money from the sale of your designs, and Sheila spends a couple of weeks each season marketing your designs. Do you see the common denominator here? Everything revolves around your designs. Meanwhile, you're at the warehouse twelve to eighteen hours a day designing the clothes and overseeing their production, and all of these women get wealthier."

"Stop!" she shouted. "We all work hard to push the line. It's a team effort. I don't know the first thing about marketing or public relations. I can't be in the store selling because I'm designing, and I have no time to model the clothes. If there aren't enough hours in the day to do my part now, how am I supposed to do everyone else's part too? You're not making any sense. We've had this conversation before and we always come back to the same place."

"I have a solution," he offered. "Consider the offer I made before you moved here. I can take over the day-to-day operation, sales and marketing while you focus on your designs. I'll hire a team to assist you in getting your ideas on paper. You can oversee the assistants, spend less time at the warehouse and produce more designs for your line."

Emily was hurt and confused. "Maybe you don't understand how this works. I design the items for my own line not some assistant."

Heath was frustrated and Emily wanted the conversation to stop. His persistence was breeding resentment toward the others because he was right and her life consisted of working late hours and being home alone from shear exhaustion. Tears were falling from her eyes as he took her in his arms and carried her to bed where he held her crying until she slept.

The next morning he was gone and atop his pillow was a note. "Returning to New York for an early meeting. Will call you later. I love you."

Emily couldn't get his words out of her head. She called a meeting for that night. It was time she stood up for herself.

◆　◆　◆　◆　◆　◆　◆　◆

When they were all gathered at the boutique, Emily conveyed her sentiments echoing the words Heath Vanderbilt had put in her head. She didn't dare tell them that he was the one responsible for her new attitude. Instead, she insisted their agreement be revised to award her more equity in the business. She held nothing back and her words stung. She belittled their individual involvement and spewed anger about them benefitting from her designs while she did most of the work. She even suggested changing the name of *Quei Forti* and making herself the focal point.

They were angry and hurt. Once the initial shock wore off, fear developed. Months and months of sweat and tears were poured into the company. At this point in *Quei Forti's* existence, a new designer was not an option. True, Emily was a very special ingredient in their recipe for success but no recipe works unless all of the ingredients are present. They had a bond that they'd come to rely on and respect. A new designer just wasn't an option nor was changing the company's name. Afraid to say something they might regret, tongues were tied until Cassie could be silent no more.

"Speaking strictly for myself now," she began, "I'm blown away. I don't even know where to begin so I won't. We all listened to what you had to say and now I think we need time, time to digest, time to think, and time to calm down."

Her sentiments went uncontested. They said their goodbyes and left Emily sitting alone wondering what she'd just done. Doubt was now in the forefront of the alliance.

◆ ◆ ◆ ◆ ◆ ◆ ◆ ◆

In the days that followed, Sunny took Emily's words to heart. While Camille was alive she traveled to fashion shows worldwide and met with various designers to secure the most sought after creations. She supplied three major boutiques in Washington, South Beach and Beverly Hills with the most exquisite pieces of fashion. The prestige was gone and her job was now reduced to running the day-to-day operations of one boutique with the added limitation of backing only one designer. Maybe Emily was right. Perhaps it would be better if she went back to running her own boutique, back to traveling, back to merchandising and back to hobnobbing with the rich and famous.

It certainly was more exciting than her life had become in recent months.

Unlike Emily and Liora, Sunny didn't have that special someone in her life. She'd occasionally dated but no one ignited a spark. She was frequenting bars and nightclubs to avoid the isolation of going home alone. Often she was asked to leave as the lights came up and the bars closed down. Once home in bed, she usually cried herself to sleep wondering if love would ever come. In the clear light of day all that remained was regret.

Inevitably, the change in her behavior was noticed. Since she worked closest with Sunny at the boutique, Cassie was the first to suspect trouble. On more than one occasion Sunny wreaked of stale alcohol from the previous night's partying. She shared her concern with Sheila and Liora, insisting that Sunny was hurt the most by Emily's accusations. It wasn't easy for Sunny to bring them all together after Camille's death and she personally invested a lot of money in *Quei Forti*. Her role was devalued by Emily's comments and Sunny was easing her pain the only way she knew how. They disagreed with Cassie suggesting she let it go.

Sheila understood Sunny's need for human contact. They were all developing lives separate from the others and trips to *The Gathering* for happy hour were less frequent. From time to time, she stopped in to say hello to Mickey and have a quick drink for companionship.

Liora also sensed they were growing apart. She reflected on her contribution to that end as she and Troy carried on their affair in secret. Going out in public was out of the question.

"It was risky enough the couple of times we went out in the beginning," Troy warned. "I just can't take the chance anymore."

Each night was spent at home waiting for Troy to tell her he'd filed the divorce papers. She ached to share her secret with the girls and seek their advice about her predicament but she knew they wouldn't understand or approve of how long she'd let it go on. Secrets, demands, drinking, and guilt; Liora was saddened by the reality of what their lives had become.

◆　◆　◆　◆　◆　◆　◆　◆

Sheila was hoping that given time, Emily would change her mind and the whole mess would blow over. Tonight she related to Sunny because she couldn't bring herself to go home alone so she went to see Mickey.

It was a quiet night at the bar. Mickey and Sheila were friends and often engaged in conversation when she stopped in for a drink. His personality was similar to Coach's at *Haute Craze* and he was easy to talk to about everything. When she arrived Mickey was engaged in conversation with a male customer down at the other end of the bar. Curiosity grew as the two glanced over at her several times. Mickey signaled he would be right down to attend to her order and then as if reading her mind, the gentleman stood from his stool and made his way to where she was sitting. From behind the bar, Mickey introduced them.

"Troy," he began, "this is Sheila."

Extending his hand Troy responded, "It's nice to meet you Sheila. My name is Troy. May I buy you a drink?"

"That would be nice," Sheila accepted, "I'll have a Chardonnay Mickey."

After depositing her wine on the bar top, Mickey left to attend to other customers. Sheila and Troy engaged in casual conversation for over an hour. She pondered the perfect timing of this meeting as she was hoping for a distraction from recent developments with her friends. Troy was charming, suave and attentive—the perfect distraction—but something about this man was unsettling. He had an odd aura and she detected a scent of almond. She declined his offer for dinner and said her goodbyes. Before leaving she spoke to Mickey about his connection to Troy.

"No connection," Mickey admitted. "He's just a customer who comes in every now and then and he seemed like a nice guy. He noticed you and since I've never seen you in here with a man, I didn't see any harm in introducing the two of you. Sorry if I overstepped."

"Not at all," she assured. "He's just not my type. Good night."

"Good night honey. Be safe," he added.

Hearing the phone ringing inside, Sheila wrestled with her keys to unlock her apartment door.

◆　◆　◆　◆　◆　◆　◆　◆

Cassie was frustrated with everyone these days. Sunny was drinking too much but Sheila and Liora were not taking it seriously. Since none of the others were taking steps to hold the group together, Cassie assumed that role. They'd worked much too hard and much too long to throw it all away now. This might be just a bump in the road but unless someone stepped up to bring them back together, one by one they would break away and *Quei Forti* would be finished.

"I'll get Sunny to help me," she thought. She convinced herself that if Sunny believed she was needed to help keep things from unraveling, she'd shift her focus away from the drinking.

Cassie arrived at Sunny's townhouse just after six o'clock. She knocked on the door and rang the bell but got no response. Using Sunny's hide-a-key, she let herself into the house while repeatedly calling her name. After checking each room and ensuring no one was home, she left on a mission to find her.

The cab driver agreed to wait outside each establishment until Cassie returned to either cut him loose or journey on to the next stop. Several clubs later, Cassie found Sunny and signaled for the driver to leave. She expected that Sunny might need a few cups of coffee before escorting her home. What she found was a dangerous predicament much like the one she encountered in New York. Sunny had obviously been drinking a lot and could barely hold her head up off the bar. From the looks of the characters groping at her, Cassie's first thought was to remove Sunny from the bar immediately.

She approached the group apologetically insisting it was time for Sunny to leave. Sunny spouted words of disappointment and insults that referred to Cassie being a party pooper. However with little steam left to resist, she got up off the barstool and allowed Cassie to support her inebriated body to the door. One of the men followed them outside while the others went back to partying. Feeling a sense of déjà vu, Cassie eased Sunny down onto the sidewalk while she dealt with the loser.

Before she could react, the guy grabbed hold of her hair and slammed her onto the cement. He repeatedly kicked her in the side while on the ground and punched her face and eyes a number of times. Outside the bar was deserted and by the time Sunny realized what was happening and got up off the ground, it was too late to help Cassie.

A woman exiting the bar scared off the attacker and called an ambulance. Help arrived quickly. Sunny was beside herself with panic but because of her condition, she was making the situation worse. The paramedics allowed her to ride along with Cassie because they feared if she tried to drive to the hospital it would be certain death for her or an innocent victim.

This time Sunny made the calls. When they came together in the hospital again all doubts, all anger and all selfishness were gone because one of them was in trouble. Nothing else mattered when a friend was hurt.

The doctor listed Cassie in fair condition recovering from a concussion, broken ribs, broken nose and a lacerated liver. He added that it would be awhile before knowing if Cassie would need plastic surgery to repair the damage to her face.

Sheila was angry at Sunny but mostly she was angry with herself for not believing Cassie. It was obvious now that she was right and Sunny needed help. Watching Sheila hurriedly walk away, Liora called after her, "Where are you going?"

"I need a minute alone," she replied. "I'm just going down the hall."

While in the waiting room trying to control her anger, Sheila looked up at the television set mounted on the wall. The network had just cut in with a breaking news story of a man wanted for rape and murder. The victim was unable to identify her assailant before she died because he wore a dark jacket with a hood that covered his face. However, she did recall a distinctive almond smell on his body. Sheila could only surmise that it was coincidence. What were the odds that the man Mickey introduced her to that same night could be this man wanted for rape and murder?

CHAPTER 12

Cassie's injuries were healing nicely and the doctor ruled out plastic surgery for now. While she was recovering, no one broached the subject of Emily's demands. Aside from feeling bad about what happened to Cassie, they each were dealing with the guilt over their role in the attack. Sheila and Liora were fighting demons for not believing Cassie. Emily concluded that none of this would be happening if she hadn't let Heath get to her. After all, hers was the spark that lit the fire under Sunny's drinking. After contemplating her actions, she realized the success of *Quei Forti* stemmed from all of them working together not just her designs. Sunny carried the heaviest burden over creating the scenario that led to Cassie being harmed in the first place.

Emily pondered her recent behavior as the words from that night echoed in her mind. She'd been dealing with an upset stomach and fatigue for days, and now she couldn't shake a vicious headache. The pregnancy test sitting on the edge of the bathroom sink would reveal whether her suspicions were correct. She was about to take something for the pain when the outside intercom buzzed. Resting the bottle of pain reliever on the counter she answered the call.

"Hi Honey, it's me," announced Heath. "I'm in town for a meeting. Surprise! Are you going to let me in?"

"Come on up," she invited.

Seeing Heath now was the last thing Emily needed as she was still tormented by the attack on Cassie and his role in that night. But if her suspicions were correct and she was pregnant, she would have to tell him in person. Anger or no anger, there's no time like the present to learn if he fathered a child.

Heath picked her up and spun her around declaring his love. After sharing a long, deep passionate kiss he proclaimed, "It's getting harder to stay away."

Staring into his eyes she declared, "I love you, too. So much has happened since you left. I wanted to call you right away but thought it best to tell you in person."

She apprised him of the attack on Cassie outside the bar and how she was trying to help Sunny, who apparently had developed a drinking problem. She confessed her guilt for taking his advice and standing up for herself which, in turn, triggered the events leading up to the attack. He listened calmly while she unburdened her conscience. When she finished, it was his turn to speak.

"It sounds to me like Sunny's drinking started long before you spoke up," he defended. "Your heart breaks for your friends' pain and you're filled with regret for what you perceive to be selfishness but you women take yourselves too seriously. A friend drank too much one night and another friend had the unfortunate luck of getting hurt while trying to help her. Cassie is okay now and what happened is in the past. Why can't you let it go and move forward? I'm more interested in what resulted from the meeting? Did they give in to your demands?"

"You selfish bastard," she shouted. "One of my best friends was so badly beaten that she had to be taken to the hospital in an ambulance. Another is spiraling out of control and all you care about is whether they gave in to my demands. These are my best friends. I thought you understood what that means to me; we are *always* there for each other. If one gets hurt or needs help, we don't hesitate. We drop everything because nothing is more important than a friend."

"Not even us?" he asked.

"Apparently not," she answered. "After all the time we've been together, if you can't respect what those women mean to me then maybe we shouldn't be together."

Heath detested taking the back seat to anyone. "Get over yourself, Emily. If any of them had a chance-of-a-lifetime shot at success but had to take it alone, you don't think they would? You're not being realistic.

That's how the world works. Smarten up before you lose everything, especially me."

"Get out!" she shouted. "We're done."

"You're not serious?" he questioned. "If I walk out that door, we're finished. I won't be coming back."

"I've been torturing myself over what I said to them and I'm appalled that you can't see how wrong I was to hurt them like that. I don't want someone like you muddying up my life. Please leave and keep your promise, don't ever come back."

Leaning against the door, Emily slid to the floor weeping. What had she done? What if she was pregnant? She just ended her relationship with the father of her baby.

◆ ◆ ◆ ◆ ◆ ◆ ◆ ◆

Unfortunately for everyone, Sunny's guilt drove her to drink even more. Sheila realized her behavior was out of control and wanted to help. However, relief wouldn't come unless Sunny acknowledged a problem existed. Believing Sunny might receive an individual suggestion to seek counseling she arranged some time alone with her by inviting Sunny to dinner. Sunny arrived on time for their seven o'clock date. As she walked passed Sheila, alcohol was present on her breath. Her staggering was another indication she had already been drinking.

"You smell like a brewery," Sheila barked.

Sarcastically Sunny responded, "Well hello to you, too. I didn't realize this was an AA meeting."

"Your drinking has gotten out of hand," Sheila advised. "I didn't want tonight to start off this way but you leave me no choice. Cassie was hospitalized because you can't control your drinking. Doesn't that mean anything to you?"

Staring back with hurt in her eyes, she defended, "I never asked her to come looking for me. If she had just minded her own business, none of it would have happened."

Sheila pleaded with Sunny to listen. "She was trying to keep you from doing something stupid. She's your friend and she loves you. We all love you."

"If you want to help," Sunny continued, "mind your own business."

"I can't," Sheila refused. "That's what friends do for each other, especially when one is in trouble. If you can't see that your life is unmanageable then maybe you need help."

"I don't need help," she denied.

"Maybe counseling," Sheila suggested. "You could talk to a professional and get some unbiased advice and see that you're throwing your life away. You'll never find peace at the bottom of a bottle. Please get help before you hurt someone else or worse yet, before you kill yourself."

"You've got some nerve," Sunny responded. "You're all judging me because I drink a little? I'm sorry if my behavior doesn't meet with your approval. I know my job at *Quei Forti* isn't as glamorous as Emily's or Liora's. I'm sorry I can't spin a campaign or handle public relations interviews like you can. I'm sorry I can't put together a social event like Cassie does. My job may not be as fascinating, but I come to work everyday and run that boutique while the rest of you soak up the glory for what you do. So I drink a little. I indulge a little. It's not out of control and I can stop whenever I want. I don't need any help. What I need is for my holier than thou friends to back off and let me live my life the way I want to live it."

"You sound ridiculous Sunny," she replied. "We are not holier than thou and our jobs are not any more glamorous than your job. Why do you diminish your role in the company? Why don't you see that none of this works unless we all do our part? You and Emily both need to wake up and stop feeling sorry for yourselves. You're being selfish and the only thing you're accomplishing is the demise of a company that we've all worked really hard to build. Fucking snap out of it, will ya? Let's go. We're going out."

"Out where?" Sunny asked. "You're not taking me to an AA meeting?"

"Nope, I'm not," Sheila confirmed. "You are the only one that can decide if that's what you need. We're going somewhere else and you need to sober up."

◆ ◆ ◆ ◆ ◆ ◆ ◆ ◆

Troy's divorce was not progressing. Liora was growing impatient with their secret affair and doubting his commitment to her. She wondered if he sincerely intended to divorce his wife at all. In her heart, time was of the essence and she had to take a stand for nothing less than total disclosure.

"Why is this taking so long?" she questioned. "We've been living this secret for months and you still haven't filed the divorce papers."

"Are we going to have this argument again?" he asked in frustration. "We've been over this numerous times and I give you the same answer each time. My lawyers are working on it and they don't think the time is right yet. I pay them to advise me so I follow that advice."

"Your lawyers aren't living this lie. I'm tired of sneaking around behind closed doors waiting for you to be free. I hate keeping secrets, especially from my girlfriends. Forcing me to keep this secret cheapens my relationship with you and them. I feel dirty and can't live with myself anymore."

Troy took Liora in his arms. "You're not my dirty little secret. I'm honored that you love me and I want to tell the whole world but I need more time," he pleaded.

"How long?" she demanded.

"Damn it!" he shouted. "I don't know how long. Stop pressing. It will happen when it happens."

"That's not good enough anymore," she confessed. "I think we should stop seeing each other until we can be open about our relationship."

"That's not an option," he insisted. "You're mine and I'm not giving you up."

"Are you not hearing me? It doesn't work for me anymore," she refused. "First of all, I'm not yours. I'm my own person and I'm done letting you call the shots. You never intended to divorce your wife, did you?"

Liora saw the anger on Troy's face so she asked him to leave. He picked up the glass on the table and hailed it across the room shattering it into pieces.

"I asked you to leave," she repeated. "Don't call me or come over anymore. A clean break is best and . . ."

Before Liora could finish her sentence, he crossed the line. Troy demonstrated the power behind his temper when he struck her across the face with the back of his hand jolting her head to the side. The substantial pain in her cheek and jaw indicated the slap would leave a bruise and the swollen lip erupting would be unsightly as well. The humiliation and helplessness that followed caused her to fear for her safety when he threatened to rape her.

"You son of a bitch, I will scream," she warned. "I'll scream louder than you've ever heard anyone scream. Unless you want to explain my face, I suggest you get the hell out of my house and never come back."

Troy stood motionless daring her to follow through on her threat.

"Now!" she screamed. "Get out!"

He knew if she screamed again someone would come to her aid and all of his efforts these passed months would be for nothing. She mustn't find out the truth.

"I'll go but this is not the end," he vowed.

The ice numbed the pain somewhat but her bruises, fat lip, and black eye could not be hidden. Disgusted by her pathetic reflection in the mirror, it was obvious she had to falsify how she got the injuries. Liora was good at spinning lies but if the others ever learned the truth, she feared the embarrassment would be worse. It was best to say she came home to find an intruder in the house. The negative publicity for *Quei Forti* was her excuse not to report it to the police. She had to make it work because she believed her life depended on it.

Liora was startled back to reality by a knock at the door. She stood paralyzed in the bathroom fearing Troy had returned to carry out his threats. There was a second knock followed by the sound of Sheila's voice calling out to her. Liora pulled herself together determined to sell this lie to her friends.

"Hey, what took so long?" asked Sheila as she heard the jiggling of the door handle. She gasped in horror when she saw Liora's face. Sunny blurted, "What the fuck happened to you?"

Liora convincingly told her story of coming home to find a man in her house. She couldn't escape before he grabbed her and slapped her across the face leaving the painfully obvious bruises.

"When did this happen? Have you called the police? Why didn't you call us?" Sheila's questions were firing faster than Liora could answer them.

"It happened about an hour ago and no I didn't call the police. The media frenzy would be a nightmare for *Quei Forti*. You of all people should understand that Sheila. I was going to call you after I took care of my face. It looks worse than it is," she assured.

"What is going on with everyone?" Sheila asked. "You're all coming apart at the seams. Is there anything we can do for you?"

"I could use help cleaning up the mess," Liora suggested pointing toward the window. "There's some broken glass over there on the floor. Can you pick that up for me? And you can stop looking at me like I just walked out of a horror movie. I feel bad enough and the two of you staring at me is creepy.

Sheila apologized with a hug then went to the window to pick up the broken glass.

"What is that weird smell?" asked Sunny.

Liora could not identify the smell and suggested it must have been something the intruder was wearing. Sheila stopped picking up the glass to concentrate on the smell. It was so familiar. The tiny hairs on the back of her neck stood up as she realized Liora's intruder might be the man on the news broadcast.

"When Cassie was in the hospital I saw a news report about a man wanted for rape and murder," she informed them. "The victim could not identify the guy but before she died she told the police he had a strange smell, like almonds. Earlier that night Mickey introduced me to a man who also smelled like almonds but I brushed it off as coincidence. Now an intruder attacks you in your home and the place smells like almonds. I think that guy is the same one who attacked you Liora. His name was Troy. Ring any bells?"

Liora's face turned ghost white and Sheila had her answer. "You have to call the police," she insisted.

"No!" Liora exclaimed. "This is crazy. I don't want to get the police involved. I'm embarrassed enough. Besides, how does a person smell like almonds?"

Sunny was standing off to the side watching Sheila's ridiculous paranoia unfold.

"She doesn't want to get the police involved," Sunny reiterated. "Why can't you just let it go? For God's sake Sheila, get a life. You're so up in everyone's face about what they should do and how they should be handling their business."

Surprised at Sunny's outburst, Liora glanced at Sheila.

"She's been drinking," Sheila explained. "That's why we're here. I needed reinforcements to convince her she needs help."

"Oh, we're back to me again," blurted Sunny. "I told you earlier that I'm fine and don't need any help. From the looks of things here, I'd say Liora is the one with the problem."

"You're right," conceded Sheila. "Since neither of you want my help I'll leave it alone. This is bullshit anyway. You're drowning in self-pity," she directed at Sunny, "and you're in denial about what happened here tonight Liora. Let's just clean up this mess and be done with it."

"Don't be that way," pleaded Liora. "I appreciate your concern but I'm really okay. The bruises will heal and I've been thinking about moving anyway. This will get me motivated to do it sooner. In the meantime, let's stop fighting before one of us says something we can't take back."

They agreed to let it go for the night but Sheila knew there was more to the story than Liora was admitting. Sunny got some fresh ice for Liora's face and Sheila went back to cleaning up the glass. As she was finishing, something shiny caught her eye. She reached over and picked up a medallion. She recognized the design and knew exactly where she had seen it before tonight. Sheila would save that conversation with Liora for another day. For now, she placed it in her pocket for safekeeping.

♦ ♦ ♦ ♦ ♦ ♦ ♦ ♦

The significant swelling under her eyes was proof of the restlessness Sheila suffered the previous night. There was no doubt in her mind that Liora's intruder was the same man she met at *The Gathering* and quite possibly the same man wanted for raping and murdering that woman. After applying as much cream as possible to cover the bags under her eyes, she dressed and headed to Liora's apartment.

"How's the face today?" she asked.

"It stings but I'll be good as new in a couple of days," she encouraged.

"Please listen to me Liora," she pleaded. "The investigative journalist in me is kicking into high gear on this one. The man that attacked you last night is definitely the man I met at Mickey's and most likely the same man the police are looking for in that rape and murder case."

Liora was frustrated with Sheila's insistence. "You don't stop, do you? I think your imagination is working overtime on this one."

Sheila removed the medallion from her pocket. Liora recognized it immediately as the one Troy always wore. It must have broken off during their argument. Again her face turned ghost white.

"If this is all in my head," Sheila continued, "then why did your face just go pale? I found this medallion on the floor last night near the broken glass. The man Mickey introduced me to at *The Gathering* had the same medallion hanging around his neck. When I mentioned his name last night, you reacted the same way you did today about the medallion. So let's stop playing games and tell me the truth. This is serious. I think your life is in danger."

Liora couldn't get passed the embarrassment of the last few months. As if things weren't bad enough already, now it seems she was having an affair with a killer. She still couldn't voice the truth. Instead, the self-loathing in her gut erupted as anger toward Sheila.

"Sunny is right about you," she began. "You involve yourself in everyone else's business because you have no life of your own. Now you want to turn a simple home invasion into a murder scenario. I have always been an only child and I like it that way. I never asked for a big sister but you keep insinuating yourself into my life as if you need to protect me. Maybe you're better suited as a mystery writer than a public relations director. Please stay out of my life and get one of your own. I think we're done here and I need you to leave."

The sting from her words hurt Sheila to the core but more so she was frightened for her friend's safety. First Sunny won't listen to reason and now Liora is doing the same. She was running out of allies. Cassie was still recovering so that left Emily.

◆　◆　◆　◆　◆　◆　◆　◆

Sunny, convinced Sheila was distracted by Liora's drama, went to the boutique to open the shop for the day. Business was slow and she was growing increasingly antsy. Since boredom from recuperation had already set in, Cassie offered to start back to work with short shifts and was more than willing to close *Quei Forti* while Sunny left to run errands.

Her favorite watering holes were no longer an option for Sunny if she didn't want the others tracking her down. To take the edge off the day, she made a quick stop at a local pub on her way out of town. Several drinks and an hour later she got in her car and with no destination in mind headed west on Interstate 66.

Reading the signs along the way, she picked a town where no one would think to look for her. "Middleburg," she said out loud. "That sounds like a nice place to visit." Meandering her way through town she came upon *Maxwell's*. She parked the car and entered the dimly lit pub that offered great atmosphere to locals.

"Perfect," she said out loud. "I can peacefully sit down for a few cocktails without anyone bothering me."

Six hours passed before Sunny left *Maxwell's*. She slid behind the wheel of the car and drove back to the interstate. Disoriented by the unfamiliar surroundings, she pulled into a rest area. Her eyes were heavy. She decided to take a short nap before finishing her journey home. She awoke in her car to the rising sun. A check of the clock on her dashboard revealed it was seven o'clock. Events of the previous day were blurry and she had no recollection of driving to the rest area. In a panicked state and realizing the others might be looking for her she put the car in reverse and backed out of her parking space. She headed home to clean up before going to work.

Fifteen minutes late and out of breath from rushing, Sunny found Emily in the office crying. Emily had already seen her come in so it was too late to sneak out.

"What brings you here so early in the morning?" asked Sunny.

"I've got a problem and need some advice," Emily confessed. "Do you have a few minutes?"

Hesitantly, Sunny sat down to give Emily her full attention. The splitting headache she was sporting made her think twice but she couldn't confess the pounding in her brain without admitting she went on a binge.

Emily communicated the details surrounding her breakup with Heath. She left out the part about Sunny's drinking so as not to spark an argument with her. When she was done unloading, the pregnancy was revealed.

"I'm really confused," she confessed. "I allowed Heath to convince me I was better off in business for myself. Once I realized his selfishness was the driving motivation, it was too late. I learned about the baby the night we broke up. Now I don't know what to do. This innocent little baby has nothing to do with what happened between us. Honestly though, I don't think I'm ready for a child in my life."

Still high from last night's binge and stumbling on her words, Sunny blurted, "Here we go again. First you want out of *Quei Forti* because you think we're taking advantage of you and now this. Don't you ever get tired of all the drama in your life? It's always one thing after another with all of you. And you all wonder why I drink. It's a hell of a lot easier to drink than deal with all of this drama."

Looking up through tear soaked eyes, Emily asked, "Are you drunk now? What the hell is wrong with you Sunny? It's ten o'clock in the morning. You're acting like a jerk. Go home and sober up. I'll handle things here."

"Right, so you can tell the others that you had to send me home because I was drinking? For your information, I have not had a single drink this morning. I'm just a little tired from last night."

Sunny saw the surprised look on Emily's face and before Emily could pass judgment, she added, "What I do on my own time is my business."

"Tired? Is that what you're calling it these days? Think what you want Sunny. You're out of control and in no shape to work with clients today. Go home."

Emily stood to walk away. Sunny lunged from her chair and grabbed her by the arm. Losing her balance, Emily fell to the floor. Angered, after just revealing she was pregnant, she got back on her feet and in Sunny's face. The argument heated up and they were shouting. Sunny, annoyed by the accusations, pushed Emily back from her face causing her to stumble again.

Emily refused to listen to Sunny's justification for her behavior. Regardless of intent or decisions left unmade, the well being of her unborn child was just put in jeopardy. Without thought, the words spilled from Emily's lips, "I'm done with this group. I should have gone out on my own when I had the chance," she screamed. "Go home Sunny. You're done here."

Sunny walked away leaving Emily alone in the office.

◆　◆　◆　◆　◆　◆　◆　◆

Sheila had driven to the warehouse in Baltimore only to learn that Emily was not coming to work. She headed back to the city and decided to swing by the boutique since she hadn't spoken to Sunny in two days. She was surprised to see Emily in the office.

"I just drove to the warehouse looking for you," she informed. "Taking the day off?"

"I came to *Quei Forti* to talk to Sunny about a personal matter," she replied. "But I didn't expect to find her smashed."

Emily explained that after confiding her problem to Sunny, she went off on Emily about everyone's drama.

"As soon as she started speaking, her breath smelled of alcohol and I told her so," admitted Emily. "I accused her of drinking already and it escalated to an argument. When I tried to leave, she grabbed my arm and I lost my balance and fell. I was pissed after what I'd just confided in her so I got in her face and we were both shouting. She pushed me away and I lost my balance and fell again."

Sheila couldn't believe what she was hearing. They were all unraveling and everything they'd worked so hard to build was crumbling down around them.

"What set her off?" Sheila asked. "I know she's been a little touchy lately but was something said that made her react so harshly?"

"As I said I needed some advice on a personal matter and I guess she didn't like what I said," Emily stated.

"What did you say to her Emily?" Sheila pressed.

"I'm pregnant," she blurted. "The night I learned about the baby, Heath and I had a huge fight. Before I had a chance to tell him I was pregnant, we broke up and he left. Now I'm pregnant and I don't want to have a baby alone. I was hoping to get another perspective on my situation so I came down here looking for Sunny."

Sheila was shocked. "Pregnant," she reiterated. "That's huge. I'm not Sunny but if you still want to talk, I'll listen."

"I'm dealing with so many emotions right now," she began. "Heath acted like an asshole insulting our friendship. He surprised me when he showed up that night because he wasn't expected for another week. I had just taken the test and didn't even know the results when he buzzed the intercom at my front door."

"So he doesn't know about the pregnancy yet?" Sheila asked.

"Nope and I don't plan to tell him either," she admitted. "I've always wanted kids but not this way, not without a father. I'm worried about the damage I've caused to *Quei Forti*, too. What should be a blessing in my life is a nightmare."

"*Quei Forti* will be fine," she assured. "We have a few problems but we'll work them out. We always do. Right now I'm worried about you. How do you feel about the baby?"

"Would you think less of me if I said I want to terminate this pregnancy?" she asked.

Sheila went away in her thoughts. Emily could sense she was somewhere else and pressed her to explain.

Sheila started rambling. "Emily, irony is a very funny thing. In the short time that we've all known each other so much has happened. Lately I've started thinking about my life in California before *Haute Craze* and *Quei Forti*. Life is all about decisions. Sometimes we make the right ones and we are better for them. Sometimes we think we're making the right decision in that moment but it turns out to be a mistake later. I'm going to share something with you that I've never told anyone. It might help with your decision so you don't make the same mistake I made."

With surprise in her voice she questioned, "You were pregnant?"

"Back in college," she admitted. "I went to a party with my roommate Trina who had a crush on some guy from the neighboring campus. I was never comfortable with the party scene so we agreed to stay together. As the night wore on, I got more comfortable with some of the guys and Trina was hitting it off with Mark. A bunch of us were playing pool and drinking. At some point in the night, I became disoriented and went looking for her. That's the last thing I remember. The following morning she said they found me in one of the bedrooms naked. I had no memory of it then and I still can't remember today."

Emily was confused. "I'm really sorry that happened to you but I don't understand what it has to do with my situation."

"Hang on, I'm getting there," Sheila assured. "The only explanation that made any sense was that someone slipped me a date rape drug, probably Rohypnol or something similar. Two days before we left school for the Thanksgiving holiday I learned of my pregnancy. I couldn't claim rape because I didn't remember anything and my family would never understand how I let something like this happen. I don't even know who it was that raped me. I have my suspicions, but could never prove it. Just like you I was tormented. I finished college a month later and went to San Francisco to have the baby."

Emily was shocked to learn that Sheila, who prided herself on full disclosure with her girlfriends, was hiding such an explosive secret. Disappointed that she had not shared this before now Emily asked, "What happened to the baby?"

"I was young and foolish thinking I could raise her on my own. I made very little money as a research assistant for the paper and I was living in a studio apartment. I got romantically involved with a pressman from the production department and he helped me find a couple to adopt her. Not one day goes by that I don't think of her and wonder where she is today. What does she look like? Did the people who adopted her give her lots of love? Does she hate me for giving her up? Even though she wasn't with me all these years, I still worried about her. Even though my heart was breaking, I believed adoption was best for her. That was then. Lately I've been thinking that I want to find her and see for myself that she's okay."

With tears in her eyes, Emily embraced Sheila and the two had a good cry.

"I guess what I'm trying to tell you," she continued "is that no matter what decision you make now it has to be one that's best for your baby, and one that you can live with for the rest of your life. Don't make any rash decisions. Give yourself time to accept the idea of a baby. Your situation is much different than mine. You have a successful career and are financially set to care for a child. I wasn't. So much is going on with all of us right now. Tensions are high and we're all saying things in the heat of the moment. We all need to take a step back and pull ourselves together. Once the dust settles, you might feel differently than you do right now."

More hugs and tears were shared but when the conversation was over Emily declared, "I'm sorry for your pain Sheila but I'm not you. I can't do this alone and I won't go through the suffering you just shared over never knowing what became of my child. I know what I have to do. Will you help me?"

That day one life ended and others were changed forever.

CHAPTER 13

They say time heals all wounds, at least for most people. Cassie was concerned this would not be the case for *Quei Forti*. The women continued to grow apart, each branching off into her own world. She reflected with sadness on how easily these ordinarily strong women were giving up on each other. Had they already forgotten how they stuck together through all the rough times? Did they not recognize the accomplishments, sweat and tears that brought them where they were today? It was inconceivable to accept that the end was inevitable.

The one bright spot in all the mayhem was Sunny's first step to recovering. She realized her life was spinning out of control and finally owned her truth. Unfortunately for the rest of them, it also meant she was pulling away. Sunny sought out counseling to deal with her issues but still refused to admit she was an alcoholic. She spent increasing amounts of time with her therapist but less time drinking. She resolved to figure out what path she wanted her life to go down and whether her role in *Quei Forti* was satisfying enough to continue the alliance. Many harsh words were exchanged on everyone's part and she wasn't sure if she had the capacity to forgive at this point. Sunny needed time to dissect the last few months and find a way to put the pieces of her life back together again.

Sheila and Liora were seldom in the same room together and when it was unavoidable, tensions ran high. Neither was ready to discuss their problem with any of the others. Sheila considered going to the police behind Liora's back to tell them of her suspicions. However, she knew that if she took that step, she would lose Liora's friendship forever. She decided it was better to wait until Liora came around and believed that eventually she would feel confident enough to share the truth behind whatever it was she was hiding. Liora needed more time.

Emily was coming to terms with her decision to end the pregnancy. There was no doubt in her mind that she did the right thing for her. The emotional fallout was not as easy to handle. She continually struggled with taking the life that was growing inside her. Since Sunny and Sheila already knew about the pregnancy, she saw no reason not to share it with Cassie and Liora. Not everyone was as understanding as she had hoped so Emily began isolating herself from the others after work hours.

Liora saw Emily's abortion from a unique perspective since she was adopted as a child. She couldn't understand why Emily didn't have the baby and let a couple that desperately wanted a child provide it with a loving home. But Liora didn't know what Emily knew. She didn't know about Sheila.

Since she was the only one not on the outs with any of the others, Cassie devised a plan to bring them all together again. Someone had to be the voice of reason. Someone had to save them from themselves. It was time for a vacation.

♦ ♦ ♦ ♦ ♦ ♦ ♦ ♦

Cassie invited Emily for a long weekend in New Orleans, and Liora and Sunny and Sheila. None of the women knew the others would be there. Cassie swore each to secrecy.

Emily was the first to arrive in The Big Easy. The celebratory spirit was evident during the drive from the airport to the Ritz-Carlton on the world-famous Canal Street. It was truly the most unique city she had ever seen. She envisioned the excitement of life that Mardi Gras and Jazz Fest must bring to the city.

The hotel boasted of genuine southern hospitality and flair. Sitting on the edge of the French Quarter, the Ritz provided easy access to most of the city's attractions. While checking in, she scanned the brochure for the European style spa that was once selected as a top luxury spa by *Healing Lifestyles and Spas*. She was ready to enjoy its luxurious therapeutic treatments. Cassie was catching a later flight so asked that Emily wait at the hotel until she arrived. It was a perfect opportunity to catch a nap before the weekend got underway.

Sheila was the next to arrive at the hotel. She was immediately transformed by the traditional southern surroundings. The hotel décor was that of royalty and elegance. Being well known for its antique stores, art galleries and restaurants, Sheila was anxious to see New Orleans. While waiting for her room key, she caught sight of a quaint restaurant, *On Trois,* across the lobby. She decided to get settled in her room and come back down for a glass of wine to wait for Cassie's arrival.

Getting all of the women to New Orleans without any of them knowing the others were coming was a difficult task for Cassie to achieve. She spaced out their arrivals so none of them would bump into the other. She came close to having it all blow up in her face when Liora decided to take an earlier flight. If not for the fact that they each were traveling on a different airline, Sheila and Liora might have been checking in at the same time. As the elevator doors closed on Sheila ascending to her room, Liora's taxi pulled up in front of the hotel.

Southern hospitality was no stranger to Liora. Growing up in Georgia, she had a fondness for jazz music. It was like coming home as she entered the lobby rich in traditional style. She knew Cassie was originally scheduled to arrive after her but since she took an even earlier flight, it gave her time to scope out the hotel's amenities. She never traveled without researching her destination and establishing an itinerary. While conducting the research for their weekend getaway, Liora discovered the hotel had a restaurant called *Mélange.* She was eager to reserve an early seating for some fine New Orleans cuisine and soothing sounds of jazz.

Sunny was the last to arrive in town. She was the toughest for Cassie to convince since Sunny mostly kept to herself in recent weeks. In the end, she agreed that time away from DC would be a good thing. In view of her fear of flying, she required a sedative to help relax on the flight. Her therapist believed the trip would benefit Sunny to start reconnecting so she wrote a prescription for two pills: one for the trip down and one for the trip back. Sunny hadn't quite shaken off the drowsiness from the first pill and she welcomed the opportunity to relax, shower and freshen up before Cassie arrived.

Cassie sat in the taxi outside the hotel trying to sum up the courage to get the weekend underway. If all went well, *Quei Forti* would be back. But there was always the possibility that she could lose them forever once her deception was unveiled. She took a deep breath, exited the cab and ventured into the hotel.

"Cassie Davis checking in," she declared at the front desk.

"Hello Miss Davis. Welcome to the Ritz-Carlton. We've been expecting you," the woman greeted.

"Thank you," she acknowledged. "Have my friends arrived?"

"They are all checked in and waiting for your arrival," she informed. "Shall I call their rooms to let them know you are here?"

"No thank you," she declined. "But can you please deliver one of these to each of their rooms?"

"I'll see that this is done immediately. If you'll follow the bellman, he'll take your bags to your room," the woman directed.

When Cassie entered her room, she breathed a heavy sigh of relief.

"Phase One complete," she said out loud. "Now it's time to get this party started."

She freshened up from her travel then changed and left the hotel.

◆　◆　◆　◆　◆　◆　◆　◆

"Please join me," the invitation read "for an evening of yachting beneath the stars. Dinner will be served and an overnight bag is suggested. Your expected arrival time is five o'clock . . . five thirty . . . six o'clock . . . six thirty. Please don't be late as we leave the dock at precisely seven o'clock. Love, Cassie." Once again, Cassie scheduled their arrival times to ensure that none of them saw the other.

As each woman arrived separately, she was greeted by one of the crewmembers that assisted her onboard and provided escort to a private cabin.

"Please get comfortable," the steward directed each time. "Miss Davis requests that you remain below in your cabin until someone from the crew comes to escort you topside."

As soon as the yacht was safely underway leaving no chance to disembark, each woman was escorted to meet Cassie in the living room for cocktails. They were confused by the presence of the others and it became clearly evident this was an ambush.

"Well hello ladies," greeted Cassie. "I'm glad to see you all made it safely. Please sit down and I'll explain what's going on here."

She sat first as defiant faces stared back. She gestured for them to have a seat and waited patiently for everyone to comply.

"I have instructed the captain not to return to the dock until I tell him to do so."

"What the hell is going on here?" demanded Sheila. "I accept your invitation for a weekend getaway and instead I get kidnapped aboard a yacht. This isn't funny Cassie. Tell the captain to take us back to the dock please."

"No one gets off the boat until all of us clear the air," Cassie responded. "You can sit there in silence for as long as you want. I personally can't stand the dissension anymore. So unless we start talking to get passed these problems, we're just gonna keep sailing further out to sea. We have this gorgeous yacht with a professional crew that is available to wait on us for the duration. There are drinks over there at the bar. I've asked the crew to stay away until I tell them we're done."

Liora headed to the bar. "Anyone else?" she asked. "Cassie's buying."

Accepting they were captives for now, they all followed suit. Sunny resisted the urge and settled for a sparkling water.

"Okay then, let's get started," Cassie instructed.

The silence in the room was deafening. As awkward as the moment was, Cassie refused to back down. Emily finally spoke up first then Sunny said her piece. One by one they each had their say. For hours they drank, hashed and rehashed every bone of contention encountered over the past two years.

Cassie insisted that each woman be given the floor without interruption until she got everything off her chest that she needed to say. They were allowed to rebut however only in a manner non-barraging to the others. It was working. The air was being cleared in a civil manner and Cassie was proud.

Sheila conceded they all had the right to make their own choices, even if she didn't agree with them. She agreed to curtail her interference but suggested that contrary to popular belief, her instincts were often correct.

Liora apologized for the hurtful things she said to Sheila and admitted that she enjoyed having an older sister. However, she asked that Sheila let Liora come to her for advice when she wanted it and not have Sheila force it upon her. She also asked forgiveness of Emily for insinuating her opinion regarding her choices surrounding the pregnancy and abortion.

Cassie pleaded with Sunny to absolve herself of any wrong doing for the attack outside the bar. Although Sunny's behavior led Cassie to the bar in the first place, the man who did the beating was solely responsible for her injuries. Sunny admitted she was addressing that guilt in therapy.

Emily forgave Sunny for pushing her to the floor and acknowledged it was not intentional. She asked their forgiveness for getting carried away about her importance in *Quei Forti*.

Sunny apologized for all the hurtful things she said and did to all of them. She shared with the group the progress she was making in therapy and assured them, although she expects the road to be long, she was working on her drinking. She was counting on their patience and understanding. She added that it was hard to watch them drink while she settled for sparkling water.

"We live in a world where alcohol is enjoyed and part of my recovery is to learn how to control what I do with those situations," Sunny stated. "I can drink and get drunk, I can drink responsibly or I can not drink at all. Today I choose to not drink at all."

The biggest surprise of the night came when Emily glanced over at Sheila and gestured for her to speak up. The others noticed and looked to Sheila for an explanation.

"Okay, okay," she surrendered. "What Emily is not-so-subtly trying to do is encourage me to tell you all about my daughter."

"Your what?" asked Liora.

"My daughter," she confirmed as all eyes were focused on her. "Back in college, I went to a party with my roommate. A bunch of us were hanging out upstairs drinking. At some point in the night, I became disoriented and everything after that is a blur. The next morning my roommate explained they found me naked in one of the bedrooms. To this day, I have no memory of what happened. I believe I was drugged. A few weeks later I learned I was pregnant. I finished college and went to San Francisco to have the baby. I got romantically involved with a co-worker at the newspaper and he helped me find a couple to adopt her."

"I can't believe you never said a word," Liora interrupted. "What happened to no secrets? I think this falls under the category of a whopper, don't you?"

"I gave away my daughter Liora," Sheila defended. "I'm not proud of what I did and I was afraid to see the disappointed looks that all of you are giving me right now."

Cassie spoke up, "Honey, it's not disappointment you're seeing, it's utter shock. None of us had any idea, except apparently Emily."

"I shared my story with Emily," Sheila continued "because she was going through a similar situation and she came to me for advice. How could I advise her about something so huge without sharing my own experience? I simply told Emily what happened to me and how I handled it. But I also told her about the constant torture it's been every day having to deal with not knowing what became of my daughter. Recently I started looking for her again. And while we're on the subject of secrets Liora, you haven't been truthful with us about how you got those bruises on your face. Since we're putting everything out on the table for all to know, why don't you come clean?"

Liora was shocked that Sheila would bring this up now but her resolve to stay quiet was weakened. The words coming out of her mouth were barely audible.

"I was having an affair with a married man," she whispered.

"This just keeps getting better," declared Sunny.

"Awhile back I met a man in a coffee shop," she began. "I accidentally dropped my wallet on his table and spilled coffee in his lap. I offered to pay his cleaning bill and one thing led to another. I didn't know he was married at first. That disclosure came after I was already falling in love. In hindsight I know it was all a lie, but he said it was a loveless marriage. Apparently a lot of money was involved and to avoid a costly settlement, he asked me to keep quiet about the relationship that now I realize was a dirty little affair. Anyway, I wanted to tell you but he insisted that no one could know. It went on for months and eventually I grew frustrated and gave him an ultimatum. When he still refused to go public, I broke it off. That was a big mistake. He got really angry. I mean violently angry and started throwing things in my apartment. When I asked him to leave, he backhanded me across the face. I was cleaning myself up when Sheila and Sunny showed up that night."

"Why did you lie to us?" asked Sheila.

"For the same reason you didn't tell us about your daughter," she insisted. "I was ashamed that he played me for a fool so I made up the story about the intruder to avoid embarrassment."

Sheila was fearful once again. "So this guy that I suspect is wanted for rape and murder was your lover for months?"

"Yes," confirmed Liora.

"And you didn't think that was important enough to mention when I came to you with my suspicions?" she added.

"How would you feel if someone came to you and suggested that the man you've been involved with, the man you loved was a rapist and murderer? I still can't believe Troy Welkins is capable of anything so violent."

"Not capable," Sheila shouted in frustration. "You just admitted he hit you hard enough to give you a fat lip, a black eye and bruises on your face."

"Yeah, but that's a far cry from brutally attacking a woman and killing her, don't you think?" she defended.

"But we all know it does happen," injected Cassie. "I'm living proof that there are monsters in this world who commit violent crimes against women. I think you need to stop denying that Sheila may be right."

"I know," she conceded. "But if I go to the police and tell them what happened, I'm afraid he'll come after me."

"I can go with you," offered Sheila. She directed the next statement to the others. "I met this man, too. The night Cassie was attacked outside the bar Mickey introduced me to a man. We talked for about an hour. There was something not right about him so I made an excuse to leave. But before I did, I noticed a strange almond smell on his body and a medallion he was wearing. I found that medallion in Liora's apartment the night she was attacked. But here's the kicker, I was watching the news in the hospital that night and there was a report of a man who attacked a woman, raping and killing her. Before she died, she told the police she remembered smelling almonds. That same smell was also in Liora's apartment the night she was attacked. Remember Sunny?"

"Yes," she agreed. "I faintly remember something about a smell but I was drinking that night so I can't say for sure what I smelled."

"But I can," confirmed Sheila. "And I recognized the medallion. I think we should go to the police when we get back. If this is not the same guy then we put this whole mess behind us and move forward. If it is him, you said yourself he has a nasty temper. You have to be sure he won't come back."

"Wait a second," interrupted Emily. "Stockman on our ranch used to wash with soap that smelled like almonds. It's widely used in the ranching business to remove the dirt and grime that sets into the skin. What did the medallion look like?"

"The medallion is round with arrows on either side. In the center of the circle is the letter B."

"Did you say B?" questioned Emily.

"Yeah," answered Sheila. "Why? Do you know it?"

"I think I do," she confirmed. "Do you remember when Liora was in the hospital and we had that crazy conversation about lilies?"

They nodded in recollection.

"I told you then that years ago I received a bouquet of calla lilies from a special friend. We were sneaking around on his family's grange because our parents didn't approve of the relationship. It was considered inappropriate for us to be involved because he was twenty-one and I wasn't eighteen yet. He was my first and damn, did he make my earth move!"

"Oh you hussy!" exclaimed Cassie.

"Anyway," she continued, "our parents eventually found out we'd been having sex in one of the abandoned bunkhouses on the Barea ranch. By the time it all came out, I was already losing interest in Brent. He had gotten really possessive and I was feeling smothered. My daddy was furious. He went down to the Barea stalls to confront him and educate Brent on the penalties of statutory rape. When Brent finally came to—yeah daddy hit him—he basically had two options: go to jail or move to his family's ranch in Wyoming for four years. I convinced Brent to go to Wyoming and by the time he was allowed to return to Dallas, I had already won the contest in *Haute Craze* and had moved to New York. The medallion you described sounds like the Barea Ranch Medallion. Maybe this guy Troy worked on the Barea ranch."

"Maybe," agreed Sheila. "When we get back to DC, we need to give all of this information to the police and let them investigate it. I don't think we can put this off anymore Liora. There's too much here for this to be a coincidence."

"There's something else," interrupted Emily. "During the grand opening gala for *Quei Forti*, I thought I saw Brent Barea leaving the ballroom at the end of the night. I called my daddy to see if Brent was still in Texas. He told me Brent left Texas and moved to Wyoming permanently but when he spoke to Brent's dad, he learned that Brent left Wyoming and no one knew where he was living. Brent never contacted me so I assumed if it was him I saw that night he had already left town. Liora, do you have a picture of Troy?"

Liora shook her head. "Unfortunately he was too paranoid for pictures. He was afraid his wife could use them as ammunition in the divorce if she ever suspected he was cheating. After listening to you guys going on about this, I'm wondering if there was ever a wife at all."

"It's late," Cassie announced. "There's nothing we can do about any of this tonight so let's worry about it when we get back to DC. We got a lot accomplished and I'm sure you're all as tired as I am. Rather than spend the night onboard we'll head back to the hotel. Before we go to our cabins for our bags, I have something to give each of you. I'll be right back."

Cassie returned with five crewmembers each carrying a bouquet of flowers containing a flame, stargazer, water, calla and tiger lily. She proclaimed, "These bouquets will forever be the symbol of our love and respect for each other and the promise of the unbroken bond that goes along with it."

They toasted their friendship then Emily added, "Please raise your glasses one more time. On a less serious note ladies, here's to you, here's to me, best friends we'll always be, if we ever disagree, the hell with you bitches, here's to me."

Laughter erupted. Donning a satisfied smirk of closure, the captain who was listening outside the door, instructed the crew, "I believe they are ready. Let's go home."

As the yacht sailed back to port, the women retreated to their cabins in preparation to return to the hotel. They realized that individually they were strong, but as a whole they were unbreakable, rare and richer for having each other. Once again they were bonded.

CHAPTER 14

Cassie was optimistic that the trip to New Orleans would end successfully so they all returned to DC on the same flight. They went over the details of their circumstantial evidence and agreed the first item on their agenda the next day would be to file a police report. Emily agreed to accompany Sheila and Liora to the police station to provide the information she knew about the Barea Ranch Medallion.

Sheila insisted that Liora move in with her until the police could eliminate Troy as a suspect in the crimes. She convinced her not to take the chance of being alone in her apartment in case he returned. Liora admitted that even if Troy was not involved with this whole mess, she was still afraid of his temper and thought he might make good on his threats.

She woke to the smell of fresh coffee brewing in Sheila's kitchen and instantly craved a cup. Rubbing her eyes as she emerged from the bedroom she felt relief to finally have everything out in the open. She reflected on how the secrets that were kept only augmented distrust among them and promised herself to never let anyone convince her to put up those walls again.

Sheila was already dressed enjoying her second cup of coffee when Liora appeared. The morning light was filtering through the window where Sheila sat attempting Sunday's Washington Post crossword puzzle.

"How many of those things do you actually finish?" asked Liora.

"Not that many," she confessed. "It keeps the mind sharp so I try. How are you feeling this morning?"

"Tired and scared," she admitted. "But I know we have to do this. What time is Emily meeting us at the police station?"

Sheila put down the puzzle. "She's coming here and we'll all go over together. I'm sure she's on her way."

Liora grabbed her mug and disappeared into the bedroom shouting back, "Then I'd better get ready."

Emily arrived a few minutes later ready to take on the world. She was hyped up from very little sleep the night before and a lot of coffee this morning. She confided to Sheila her concerns about Brent being in town approximately the same time Liora met Troy. Although she'd never seen Brent wear one of the ranch medallions, it was all too eerie for her.

"The sooner we get the police involved, the better we'll all sleep at night," Emily concluded.

◆ ◆ ◆ ◆ ◆ ◆ ◆ ◆

Sheila, Liora and Emily joined hands as they ascended the steps to the District of Columbia Metropolitan Police Department. The Sergeant at the front desk greeted them. Liora informed him she wanted to file a police report for an assault and Sheila added they had information on the man wanted for rape and murder. Finally, she expressed her suspicions that Liora's attacker might possibly have been the same man. The officer directed them to the seats in the waiting area while he contacted the detective on the case to come speak with them.

Sheila saw an older gentleman coming toward them hurriedly. He extended his hand offering a greeting and introduced himself as Lieutenant Jake Marcello.

"Lieutenant," acknowledged Sheila. "I'm Sheila Marmion. This is Emily Barrington and Liora Courtlandt."

"I understand you ladies have some information on a case I'm working," he stated.

"We think we do," responded Sheila. "Liora was assaulted a few weeks ago and based on the details of her attacker we think it might be the same man you're trying to find."

"This way please," he directed. "Let's go to my office and I'll take your statement Ms. Courtlandt. Then you two can tell me what you know and why you think it's my guy."

Lieutenant Marcello listened as Liora stated the events of that night. She informed him of her relationship with Troy Welkins and her desire to end that relationship which led to the assault. As the words were coming out of her mouth, she was disgusted with her gullibility over the entire affair. When she finished, it was Sheila's turn.

She began, "I had stopped in at *The Gathering* for a drink before heading home. The bartender, who I know personally, introduced me to a man named Troy. We talked for about an hour and the guy started creeping me out so I made an excuse to leave. While we were talking, I noticed a medallion he was wearing and perceived a strange hint of almond on his body. I didn't think anything of it and just wanted to go home. But later that night, a friend of ours was injured and taken to the hospital. At the hospital I saw the news story on the woman who was raped and murdered. It was reported that before she died she identified her attacker as having this strange almond odor. I didn't really believe that the man I met was the same man, but it gave me chills just the same. Anyway, it wasn't until Liora was attacked and I smelled it again in her apartment that I started to believe they were all the same man. After I found the medallion, I was convinced."

"Any why didn't you come in sooner with this information?" he asked.

Liora interrupted, "That would be my fault. I refused to believe that someone I was involved with could be a killer so I told Sheila she was crazy. She knew unless I came forward with her, there wasn't anything to corroborate what she was saying. So it was dropped. We recently took a trip with a couple other friends and while discussing some of these coincidences more information came to light."

"That's where I come in," Emily stated. "When Sheila told us that she found a medallion in Liora's apartment exactly like the one she saw on the man she knew as Troy, I asked her to describe it to me. I recognized the description as the Barea Ranch Medallion. I grew up in Texas on a ranch and the neighboring grange belonged to the

Barea family. All hands working the ranch were given a medallion, as well as each family member. So we surmised that the killer, your killer, might have worked on the Barea ranch at some point."

"That's quite an interesting story," he acknowledged.

"Wait there's more," warned Emily. "I saw Brent Barea in Washington on the night of our company's grand opening. I wasn't sure if my eyes were playing tricks on me so I called my daddy in Texas. He looked into it for me and learned that Brent was no longer in Texas. Apparently he moved to his family's ranch in Wyoming and then for reasons no one seemed to understand, he left Wyoming and no one's heard from him since. At least as of the last time I spoke to daddy."

"Interesting," he responded. "Here's what we're going to do ladies. Dig deep into your memories and write down every detail you can remember about the incident and any individuals involved; dates, times, anything that comes to mind. Give us as many details about Mr. Welkins that you can recall and his vehicle type, if he had one. Ms. Barrington, please describe this Barea Ranch Medallion and give us the names and contact information for your father and the Barea family. Make sure you include your contact information so I can follow up with you if I have any more questions. This guy is every woman's nightmare and if my guy is your guy then you need to be very careful. Ms. Courtland, is there some place you can stay until we locate Mr. Welkins?"

"I'm staying with Sheila for now," she informed. "I just need to pick up some things from my apartment on the way home."

"Great. I'll have our department artist work with you to put together a sketch based on the details you recall about Mr. Welkins," he concluded.

"Before you go," interrupted Sheila, "here is the medallion I took from Liora's apartment. It's the same as the one worn by the man I met."

"That's it," confirmed Emily. "That's the Barea Ranch Medallion."

Emily left the Lieutenant's office to make a phone call while Liora and Sheila worked with the sketch artist.

On the way home from the police station, Liora received the call she'd been dreading for months. Expecting to hear bad news concerning her mother, she was surprised to learn that her father had died from a massive heart attack. The lawyer assured her that Aline was in good hands but she was needed in Georgia to make the arrangements for her father's burial.

All of the women traveled to Georgia in support of Liora's family tragedy. Aline's advanced state of Alzheimer's prevented her from processing that Vincent had died. Once the services were concluded, Liora got her mother settled into her new home where she would receive the proper care and treatment for her disease. With great sadness and regret for not visiting more often before this progression, Liora returned to DC and the black cloud surrounding her life.

◆ ◆ ◆ ◆ ◆ ◆ ◆ ◆

Quei Forti was gearing up for the unveiling of the new line. All hands were on deck for long hours of final touches. Emily and Liora wrapped up the designs and fittings, Sunny made way for the new arrivals in the boutique, Sheila provided campaign details to the media and once again Cassie was busy planning the social event of the season. They were exhausted and barely able to stand up so Cassie suggested they break for the night and go to *The Gathering* to unwind and relax.

"I'm up for some singing," agreed Liora. "It might be fun. We haven't been out together in a long time."

"I could eat," added Sunny.

Mickey was so excited to see them all together. "Ladies, how nice of you to grace our establishment tonight," he greeted. "I know you've been busy and I'm sure that's why you haven't been in to see your favorite bartender, but I'm glad you're here now. I believe your table in the back is open. Take a seat and I'll send a round right over."

"Not for me, Mickey," Sunny corrected. "Soda water with a twist please."

"No singing tonight, Mickey?" Liora asked.

"I'm afraid not honey," he apologized. "There's always the jukebox."

It was so nice to get out together again and laugh. *Quei Forti* was back and stronger than ever. They discussed the final details for the unveiling and concluded that everything was on track and would be ready by the end of the week. The distraction was just what the doctor ordered until halfway through the meal when the television set indicated a breaking news story.

"There has been another brutal attack," the anchor informed. "Earlier tonight, a woman was found raped in the park by a jogger. The victim was taken to George Washington University Hospital but no details are available at this time regarding her condition."

The anchor continued noting the location of the park, "Authorities are warning women in the area to be extremely careful and if at all possible, do not go out alone."

Liora grew nervous. "That park is just a few blocks from here."

Sheila sprang from her chair declaring, "I'm going to the hospital. I need to speak to Lieutenant Marcello and find out if this is the same guy."

"Sheila," Liora yelled, "they just said not to go out alone. Are you crazy?"

"Then come with me," she suggested. "But I'm going with or without you."

Lieutenant Marcello was already waiting at the emergency room when they arrived. He could see the terror on their faces as they approached him in the hallway.

"Is it him?" asked Sheila.

"We think so," he confirmed. "The victim can't identify her attacker because it was dark and he was wearing a dark hooded jacket. However, she did say he wore strong cologne. She couldn't be more specific about the cologne, only that it was strong."

Sheila and Liora looked at each other. There was nothing to say. Liora knew what Sheila was already thinking. They needed protection.

Lieutenant Marcello agreed to their request. Since there appeared to be no connection between Troy Welkins and the others, he offered to have a patrol car keep an eye on Sheila's place since both she and Liora were staying together. Additionally, a car would watch Liora's apartment in case he turned up there. The sketch details provided to the police artist would be helpful in spotting him if he showed up.

"It's only a matter of time," he assured them "before he makes a mistake and we catch him. He doesn't know yet that we can identify him but he will after tonight. We've decided to broadcast the sketch on the news for the safety of the women in the city. Before I forget, here's a copy of the sketch the artist drew based on your description. Show it to your friends. If anyone recognizes this man or knows his whereabouts, contact me immediately."

"He'll know," blurted Liora. "He'll know it was me and he'll come looking for revenge."

"There's no reason for him to suspect you Ms. Courtlandt," he corrected. "There won't be any mention of your assault so he'll think the woman he attacked tonight was the one that identified him."

"He's not stupid Lieutenant," she insisted. "Once his face is plastered on the news, he'll realize that I can identify him, too."

"I'm going to have a couple of officers take you all home," he offered. "Two officers will sit outside the apartment all night so you'll be safe. Please try to relax and trust me. We will catch him."

"Wait!" shouted Emily. "I know this man. I think this is Brent Barea."

"Are you sure?" asked the Lieutenant.

"Yes," she confirmed. "Troy Welkins is Brent Barea. How is that possible?"

"This puts a whole new spin on the investigation," he warned. "If Brent Barea is the true identity of the man we are looking for, it's too much of a coincidence that he got involved with your friends. I'm assigning another patrol car to watch your home, too" he added. "Ms. Barrington you might very well be the key to solving this case. In the meantime, we'll contact his family in Texas and get a photograph for the news and hopefully a sample of his DNA for comparison to the rape kits. For now all of you go home. Let us do our job and be very careful."

Liora stared out the window as the hospital faded in the distance. The man she was having an affair with for months is the same man Emily burned and the same man her father sent to exile for years. She suspected there was more to this story than anyone understood and that life was going to get a whole lot worse before it got any better.

♦ ♦ ♦ ♦ ♦ ♦ ♦ ♦

"Did you sleep at all?" Sheila asked the next morning.

"Not a wink," Liora replied. "What about you?"

Sheila shook her head. "Do you think we should postpone the unveiling next week until this creep is caught?"

"Part of me says yes," she began "but I think we need the distraction or we'll go insane. Besides I spent months hiding because of this asshole and I refuse to hide anymore. He's targeting all of us: you, me and now Emily is involved. Once his true identity is confirmed and plastered all over the news, he'll be out for revenge. Cassie and Sunny might be at risk, too. If this guy is the same man Emily was involved with we need to draw him out before he kills anyone else. The only way to do that is to stay in the public eye."

"It's risky but okay. I think you're right," she agreed. "Let's go to work."

It was obviously a sleepless night for all of them. Liora was right and it wouldn't do any good to hide now. There was a show to put on next week and work to be done. Before tackling the business of the day, Sheila and Liora shared their concern that the others might also be in danger.

"No argument here," Cassie concurred. "This is getting really creepy so remember that we are stronger as a whole than individually. Let's agree to some basic rules to live by until this fucker is in custody. Under no circumstances do any of us venture out alone. We cut back on all social engagements except those that are imperative for us to attend, and then only if we have an escort or at least two of us attend the function together. This is the most important rule of all. Please promise to always notify the rest of us when you arrive home safely. No one sleeps until we know that everyone is home. Once inside our homes, the police are outside protecting us. This plan will work and give us all some peace of mind. I don't know about the rest of you, but my eyes can't take anymore sleepless night."

In an effort to maximize security efforts the unveiling party was scaled back to one venue. They chose the Odyssey because a cruise guaranteed restricted access and once out on the water no unwelcome guests could show up. A large security force was on hand to admit only those guests whose names were on the list. Lieutenant Marcello was onboard looking sophisticated in a penguin suit and he mingled with the other guests to avoid suspicion. Troy Welkins a.k.a. Brent Barea wouldn't dare show up to a party onboard a boat preventing any chance for escape.

The guests were unsuspecting of anything out of the ordinary. As most upscale parties in the DC area often attracted dignitaries and rich socialites, they assumed the security was for their protection.

The moon was full, the water calm and the monuments lining the shoreline leant excitement to the evening's festivities. The Odyssey set sail without incident and everyone settled down for the fashion show.

The first theme of the night was earth, wood, and stone. Brown, the color most associated with earth, was the focus of the first set of designs. Liora wore a spectacular cocoa sequined evening gown expelling wholesomeness and earthiness. In keeping with the earthy concept, elegant accent jewelry pieces in shades of green were observed.

Following her were models expressing design in lighter tones of tan, taupe, beige, and cream with accents in yellow and rusty orange. They provided an excellent emphasis to the main attraction.

The second theme was passion and love. Red, being a strong color appealing to those senses, was the focus for the next set of designs. Liora wore a satin floor length gown, long white gloves and carried a golden pitchfork suggesting a dash of daring. The models presenting backdrop designs donned shades of pink and yellow in harmony with the little devil.

The final theme of the night was flamboyance and energy. Orange, in its vibrancy, expressed the energy and warmth of the sun. Liora's fun and flirty cocktail dress offered a gathered bust and smooth waist revealing every curve of her figure. It stimulated the emotions of the gentlemen crowd as their flush cheeks indicated escalating rates of respiration and rising blood pressure. In staying with the edginess of the color, Liora's dress really popped with the other models wearing medium blues and greens.

The applause was confirming. *Quei Forti* had just unveiled another successful line of designs by Emily Barrington. Dinner was served as the band played quietly in the background. Some guests strolled along the outer deck of the boat while others took advantage of the mood and enjoyed a romantic spin around the dance floor with their loved one. Three hours later the Odyssey returned and all had a great time.

◆ ◆ ◆ ◆ ◆ ◆ ◆ ◆

Lieutenant Marcello kept his word and contacted the Barea family in Texas. No one knew of Brent's whereabouts or if they did, they were not forthcoming with any information. The family claimed they hadn't heard from him in months. His parents provided the police with recent photographs and an old toothbrush left behind when he moved to Wyoming. The DNA obtained from the toothbrush was compared to the sexual assault kits from the victims and it confirmed that Brent Barea was indeed the man responsible for the recent crimes.

Weeks went by with no new information or sightings of Brent. Fortunately, that also meant there were no new attacks on any women in the DC area. Some speculated he left town after his picture and identity were plastered all over the news. Hesitantly, the people of the nation's capitol returned to their normal routines.

The women of *Quei Forti* were not convinced he was gone. After all, he went to great lengths to insinuate himself into the lives of the people Emily loved. For that reason alone, they believed he was not done with them yet. Constant communication with each other was maintained as the police presence dwindled indicating they also believed he was no longer in the area.

"Please don't do this Lieutenant," Liora pleaded. "He's still out there and he's just waiting for you to give up. Why would a man who was scorned by a woman years ago, a man who has been so meticulous about planning his revenge, just give up and go away? It doesn't make sense. He knew he was running the risk of Emily recognizing him when he started this sick game. Now that she has I'm sure it only made him more determined and careful about his actions. It has not weakened his resolve. If anything, it probably made him more determined to see it through to the end."

"We're not giving up," he assured her. "But we can't keep patrol cars on your residences twenty four hours a day. We don't have the manpower. We're cutting back, not giving up. If he's still in DC and makes another move, we'll have clues to investigate. We have nothing right now. He hasn't attacked anyone else and no one has seen him in a month. My guess is he's moved on and will probably resurface in another city. He can't run forever."

"You better hope he doesn't resurface back here and kill one of us before you have any new clues," Liora warned.

CHAPTER 15

Quei Forti was basking in the afterglow of the unveiling party aboard the Odyssey. Requests were pouring in for designs from Emily's new line. It was hard to keep up with the demand and long hours were being worked once again as new designs had to be created. Liora and Sheila concluded a shoot with *Haute Craze* featuring the designs presented at the Odyssey show. Sunny was hard at work trying to indulge *Quei Forti's* clients coming into the boutique. Cassie was trying to keep everyone's spirits up in the wake of Brent's disappearance.

"I think a wrap party is in order," Cassie announced. "The stress over Brent's disappearance has us all wound up. We've worked really hard to launch the new line, the shoot went great and a little gratification is warranted. What else can we do when the party mood strikes, Liora wants to sing and the need to gather with friends and dance the night away arrives? Rent *The Gathering* and celebrate *Quei Forti's* best season yet."

"A little over-the-top on the speech Cassie but I think it's a great idea," agreed Liora. "A little singing, dancing, food, friends and fun sounds perfect to me."

Mickey was happy to accommodate the ladies, especially on such short notice. Invitations were hand delivered to a small group of seventy-five guests and almost everyone accepted the offer. It was time to get wild and crazy!

◆　◆　◆　◆　◆　◆　◆　◆

As always no expense was spared for this Friday night. A hostess who verified that all attendees were on the approved list greeted guests at the door. Mickey brought in a full staff including bartenders and waitresses. A top cocktail bar was open while wait staff circulated the room offering hors d'oeuvres, special champagne, and Jell-O shooters. An eclectic style of incredible food was splashed throughout the joint.

Couches were brought in, the stage had full lighting for the live band, and a giant video screen was on-hand for Karaoke entertainment pleasure between sets. A convenient dance floor was set up on the outdoor patio to merge the energy of the party with the pre-springtime night air. A fire pit, horseshoes and volleyball nets were set up for all to enjoy. It was a fantasy escape from a passionate heart for a favorite night in the city. There was nothing left to do but turn up the music and enjoy the surroundings.

Liora was in her glory. Not only was she the Karaoke queen, but also as a special treat she was invited up on stage to sing with the band. She slid up behind the microphone as applause rang out to take the lead position for *Me and Bobby McGee*. The chemistry was working well.

It was a lively, fun atmosphere and everyone was making their own vibe. The ambiance, festive mood and allure of good people guaranteed an enjoyable party with smashing success.

Cassie easily handled her role as party planner. She circulated, connected and conversed with a number of people to develop and maintain close relationships. Tonight's rapport had already been established. *Quei Forti*'s visibility was enhanced by her ability to interact with the crowd. She was wonderful at finding the one person standing in a corner of the room and easing their apparent discomfort with an opening line. But she was even better at finding two people and bringing them together in conversation. Then she would graciously end her participation with a little humor and walk away leaving them enjoying the party like everyone else.

Sunny did not fare as well as the others. Her therapist had warned her about stresses that could trigger another drinking binge. God knows there were enough stresses at work in her life right now. She was motivated to learn how to drink in moderation. Sunny was well aware what it would cost her if she started drinking heavily and blacking out again. During the first few months of therapy she adhered to total abstinence. In recent weeks she had started sipping wine but eliminated all hard alcohol as an option forever. When the urge hit to have a scotch, she reminded herself of all the idiotic and hurtful things she did when she was drunk. Alcoholics cannot drink in moderation but then Sunny never admitted to being an alcoholic. For that reason, she signed a contract with her friends permitting them to speak up if they thought she was getting out of control. Tonight she was sipping, getting her groove on, keeping it half tilt boogey and learning how to control her behavior.

Emily was working her true feminine powers on a new man. She was finally at peace with her decision to terminate the pregnancy and replaced the guilt with renewed self-respect. She was embracing her past and understanding its purpose. She no longer lived in fear of the future because of what she'd done in the past and no man would ever again define who she was as a person. Tonight she was giddy with happiness and feeling very much like a woman who found the hidden treasure within her soul. She had grace and she felt desired.

Sheila envied the outgoing personalities of the other women. She'd spent most of her adult life feeling socially misfit because singing, partying and relationships were never a real draw for her. Most often parties were fast-paced, loud and made her feel anxious but she couldn't stop because she was built to make others feel better. If that meant supporting her friends by attending a party with seventy-five people when she'd prefer to be home with a good book, then so be it. No matter how hard she tried, she always felt poorly adjusted to her social environment. It was difficult to walk that fine line between happiness and losing control. In her mind it was a formidable social battlefield. However, she was not lacking in intellectual insight so she managed to graciously converse with a smile and act like she was having the time of her life. Watching the scene unfolding before her now, she yearned to lose herself in the quest to find her daughter.

"Penny for your thoughts," offered Cassie.

"People watching," she replied, "and wondering why complete strangers walk up to me, shake my hand as if they know me then walk away without saying anything," she complained.

Cassie looked at her with that coy little smile, "They're just being friendly. It's usually best to ignore those people. Now get your butt off that barstool and join me on the dance floor."

Sheila may have felt socially inept but when it came to dancing she was fantastic. It was her way to work out and keep her body in shape. Watching her move to the beat of a song, one might think she had a previous life as a Vegas stripper. She seldom wore sexy clothes but was always seductive when she danced. Liora and Sunny watched from the sidelines as Cassie and Sheila took the dance floor.

"She dances with such confidence and attitude," Liora remarked.

"Yeah," agreed Sunny, "and look how she gets the crowd charged up. Drooling idiots. She's moving to the music like she's making slow, passionate love. Damn!" she exclaimed, "I wish I could do that."

"Lucky the man who snags her one day," complimented Liora.

As the lights came up signaling the end of the party, Liora was called back on stage for one last song of the night. She finished off the evening with a slow song for couples to wind down on the dance floor. The other women joined her on stage.

Liora passed the microphone to Cassie. "Thank you everyone for coming. Please drive safely and we'll see you at the next bash. The new Emily Barrington designs are out so if you haven't done so yet, come see us for your original. Good night."

Mickey convinced them to stick around for a nightcap while the staff cleaned up the place. It was like old times hanging out with Mickey after hours. When the clock struck two o'clock it was time to go home.

◆ ◆ ◆ ◆ ◆ ◆ ◆ ◆

Sunny, Cassie and Emily rode together since they all lived in the same direction. Sheila and Liora planned to share a cab home but Liora said she needed to go to her place to pick up some clothes.

"Now?" questioned Sheila. "It's two o'clock in the morning. Can't it wait till tomorrow?"

"Nah, I'd prefer to do it now. I'll just run up real quick and grab a few things. I've been away from my place for so long and I'm tired of the same old clothes," she defended.

"I don't think it's a good idea," warned Sheila. "We still don't know for sure that Brent is not in DC."

Holding up her thumb and finger, Liora teased, "This close."

Sheila was confused. "What are you talking about?"

"We almost went a full day without mentioning his name," she explained. "Look, I'll have the doorman escort me up to my place to make sure the coast is clear. I'll call you when I'm on my way back so you know everything's fine. Since your place is on the way, we can ride together to drop you off and then I'll grab my stuff and be back at your place in thirty minutes. I'll even ask the cab driver to stay outside so I don't have to wait for another cab."

"What if I go with you to your place and then we both go back to my place together?" she suggested.

"Because you're exhausted," Liora answered. "This would be a perfect time for you to practice being a big sister and trust me. I won't be long but I will be very careful. Now stop arguing with me and get in the cab. The meter is running."

Sheila hated this plan but knew Liora was not going to capitulate. Once she made up her mind there was no changing it. They talked about the party on the ride and both agreed it was one of Cassie's best. Ten minutes later, the cab pulled up in front of Sheila's place. Exiting the cab she pleaded one more time but Liora instructed the driver to pull away.

Up in her apartment, Sheila got a call from Sunny, Emily and Cassie to let her know they had all arrived home safely. She told them about Liora's insistence to go back to her place for clothes and refusal to let Sheila go with her. She listened quietly as they each spouted a lecture knowing it was out of Sheila's control. Liora was determined to not let Brent's unknown whereabouts make her a prisoner. Grant it, she was acting foolish to go for clothes at this hour but she was trying to prove something to herself. She wanted to take back control of her life and move about the city without fear.

Forty-five minutes passed and Sheila hadn't gotten the call from Liora. She stared out the window waiting for a cab to pull up, hoping it just slipped her mind. She wanted to honor Liora's request and stop hovering. Keeping that promise was proving hard to do as each minute passed without a call. She convinced herself to give it five more minutes then she was calling Liora.

Holding the cell phone in her hand, she paced back and forth in front of the window. The minutes ticked slowly and had it not been for the clock on the wall indicating only two minutes had passed, Sheila would have sworn it was an hour. Three . . . four . . . five but still no call. She opened the cell phone and dialed Liora's number. The phone on the other end rang five . . . six . . . seven . . . eight . . . nine . . . ten times. Then the dreaded voicemail, "Hello, you've reached Liora Courtlandt. Sorry I missed your call. Leave a message and I'll call you back."

Sheila's heart was in her throat. She called Cassie. "Liora never called. I'm heading over to her place now. Call the others then meet me there." Without waiting for a reply, Sheila hung up the phone and ran out the door.

Cassie called Sunny who then called Emily. They were all on their way.

Sheila flew out of the cab and into the lobby of Liora's apartment building.

"Bobby," she called to the doorman, "Did Liora ever come back down from her apartment after you took her upstairs?"

"I didn't take Ms. Courtlandt upstairs," he admitted. "She came in about an hour ago and said she was going up to get some things. She hasn't come back down yet."

"Do you have a key to her apartment?" Sheila asked.

"Yes I do but I can't use it when Ms. Courtlandt is in her apartment," he added.

"Come quickly," she frantically directed, "and bring that key."

The bellman followed Sheila onto the elevator. She informed Bobby that it was still not safe for Liora to be alone in her apartment and she was supposed to have him escort her upstairs and wait while she packed a few clothes. She was only supposed to be in the apartment for a few minutes and then return to Sheila's place.

"I'm not getting a good feeling here Bobby," she warned. "It's been an hour since I left her and it should not be taking this long."

Just as she finished her sentence, the elevator doors opened on Liora's floor. They ran to her apartment and Sheila gasped when she noticed the door was ajar. She flung it open calling out for Liora but there was no answer.

"Oh my God," Sheila cried. "What the fuck happened here? Liora! Liora are you here? Answer me honey. Where are you?"

The shock of Liora's ransacked apartment sent chills up Sheila's spine. They pushed aside the debris from the foyer to get into the apartment. They hadn't made it further than the kitchen when screams came from the doorway. Sunny, Cassie and Emily had just arrived and were looking at the devastation left behind in the wake of an apparent fit of rage.

"Where is she?" yelled Emily. "Where the fuck is she?"

Taking her by the shoulders Cassie sternly spoke, "This is not helping Emily. Calm down and help us find her."

She obviously was not in the living room so Sheila and Bobby went to check the bedroom while Sunny and the others checked the den and guestroom.

"This is bad Bobby," Sheila stated. "Whoever did this was very angry and . . ."

"Help," was the faint cry from near the window.

"Bobby over here," Sheila urged. "Help me move this chair. Oh my God. Liora I'm here. We're here," she assured. "Call 911 Bobby and tell them to hurry. It's a matter of life and death."

There on the floor beneath the rubble of a busted chair and broken glass was Liora lying in a pool of blood. By the time paramedics arrived five minutes later, Liora was not breathing. Sheila had already initiated CPR but stepped aside when they rushed into the room. The paramedics checked her pulse, breathing and airway then provided intravenous medication. They located the source of the wound and secured a bandage to stop the bleeding. After several minutes Liora still had not regained consciousness. They all watched in horror as she was losing all signs of life.

The Fire Department and police emergency teams also responded to the scene. The paramedics worked relentlessly for more than twenty minutes to stabilize her long enough for transport to George Washington University Hospital. Sheila insisted on riding along with her in the ambulance. On the way to the hospital, Liora's heart stopped twice. Sheila looked on as defibrillation was provided and they attempted to revive her. The paramedic pulled out his penlight to test for pupil responsiveness then urged the driver to hurry.

Outside Liora's apartment building was a frenzy of police cars. Lieutenant Marcello was pulling up in an unmarked sedan as the women were getting into a cab.

"Wait," he called out to Emily. "Get in my car. I'll take you to the hospital."

The automatic doors to the Emergency Room parted for entry as they witnessed typical Friday night chaos in a big city hospital. The waiting room was filled with patients waiting to be seen by a doctor. Lieutenant Marcello flashed his badge to the triage nurse who directed him to the double doors then buzzed him in.

"Wait here," he instructed the women. "Let me talk to the doctor and get some information on her condition."

"I don't think so," refuted Cassie. "We're the only family she has left and we're going in there with you."

By now the triage nurse had come out of her office insisting they could not go inside. It was pointless to argue and make a scene so they relinquished their demand for the time being. A couple of officers had come into the Emergency Room and Lieutenant Marcello instructed the women to go with them to give their statements. Holding on to each other in fear, they followed the officers to a small room around the corner.

The officers asked to speak with each of them separately to get details of what happened. Cassie was first to stay behind and give her statement. She explained that after the party ended, Sheila and Liora took a cab home together. Cassie told them about the conversation she had with Sheila wherein Sheila said Liora insisted on going to her place alone to pick up some clothes.

"Sheila tried to talk her out of it," Cassie said. "But Liora insisted on going alone because she was tired of hiding and living in fear of Brent Barea."

"Do you know that Mr. Barea did this to your friend?" the officer asked.

"Did I see him do it?" Cassie sarcastically asked. "No I didn't. But we all know it was him. Liora begged Lieutenant Marcello not to remove the police protection on her house and Sheila's house. She warned him something like this would happen and now she's in there fighting for her life."

Sunny gave her statement next providing the same information. Emily's story was almost verbatim to the first two. Almost an hour had passed since the detective went to check on Liora. They were frantic that he hadn't come back to report on her condition.

"Why is no one telling us anything?" Emily questioned the nurse. "How long does it take to find out what the hell is happening in there?"

"I'm sorry Miss," the nurse apologized. "But we can only give out information to immediate family. You'll have to wait until the policeman comes out to talk to you."

"But we are her family," she insisted. "Her father recently passed away and her mother is in a home with advanced Alzheimer's. There is no one else."

"I'm sorry Miss. There's nothing I can do," she replied.

Emily broke down weeping. Cassie and Sunny rushed to her aid and guided her back to their seats. She laid her head on Cassie's shoulder and cried like a baby. Before she could finish her cry, the detective returned. They rushed to him, stopping suddenly when they saw the look on his face.

"She's gone now," he advised them. "Her heart stopped twice in the ambulance on the way here. The paramedics were not able to revive her the second time. I'm very sorry for your loss."

They were devastated. With tears in her eyes Cassie denied, "It can't be true. She asked for your help. You promised to protect her. It can't be true." Liora had just died and she was angry. She wanted to punch holes in the walls and scream at the world to fuck off.

Sunny's initial reaction was raw numbness. She kept thinking to herself, "She's at peace now. No more pain."

Cries and screams were heard throughout the halls of the emergency room when Emily broke down in Cassie's arms at the thought of never seeing her friend again. She cried her heart out while they waited for Sheila to come out.

Hospital procedure mandated that someone she named as the next of kin identify Liora. After her father's fatal heart attack and her mother's rapid progression of Alzheimer's, Sheila had agreed to act as Liora's next of kin. Due to the circumstances of her death, an autopsy would be performed and although the hospital did not need permission to perform an autopsy, the courtesy of consent was extended to the next of kin. Sheila had to make a formal identification of the body and sign the paperwork for the postmortem. Liora would remain in the hospital mortuary until arrangements could be made with the funeral director.

The sun was coming up on a new morning as they exited through the automatic doors. What a horrific day!

CHAPTER 16

Sheila refused to display her emotions at the hospital. She didn't want to criticize the doctors or paramedics responsible for treating Liora. She didn't want to show weakness in front of the other women. They would look to her for strength to take care of the funeral arrangements. But she swore on her own life that she would get Brent Barea if it was the last thing she ever did.

Whitehall Funeral Home didn't open for another hour. The others were meeting her at the funeral home so she had time for a quick shower and coffee before heading down to meet them. It was a tense, traumatic time she was facing and she struggled with thoughts rushing in during this time of stress. As in social settings, Sheila was very uncomfortable with situations involving change. Her mind kept searching for an answer.

"God," she pleaded, "give me the strength to get through these next few days."

At precisely nine o'clock Sheila arrived at Whitehall's to find the others waiting for her. The main reception area appeared elegant, comfortable and gracious. They agreed on a dignified funeral ceremony and an opportunity to say good-bye to their friend. Although it would not heal the inner turmoil of their loss, it was necessary to face the forced smiles and disconnected feelings of those wishing to seek closure.

They settled on one evening's viewing for the public to pay their respects. There was an overwhelming number of people in attendance and police officers lined the streets to offer crowd control and protection from on-lookers. Lieutenant Marcello suspected that Brent Barea might try to disguise himself and get a look at his work. They would be ready for him if he showed his face. But tonight was an opportunity for family and friends to gather and remember Liora while offering comfort to those who knew her best. She was a celebrity in her own right and that was confirmed by all of those showing up to remember her.

As their black limousine pulled up to the funeral home, they witnessed a sea of paparazzi and flashing cameras. Subdued funeral guests who were dressed in black filled the place to capacity. The funeral home staff assisted in keeping the mourners flowing in an effort to allow everyone an opportunity to offer their support and comfort. This showing of love gave meaning to a special person's life.

The day after the viewing was reserved for almost one hundred of her close friends and family. A small service was officiated by a non-denominational minister as Liora always said she was spiritual but not religious.

"I don't know how to get through this," Emily confessed. "I just can't wrap my head around the fact that Liora is gone and we're burying her today. How did we let this happen? We promised Vincent and Aline we would take care of her and now she's dead."

"We take it one minute at a time," Sunny suggested. "It's the only way to get through this senseless tragedy."

Sheila approached the podium fighting to maintain composure as her legs weakened beneath her shaking body.

"This service is all about remembering Liora," she began. "Grief is a matter of the heart. We must allow ourselves to shed the tears and feel the grief. A beautiful life was cut short and we are saddened. Our mind will never let us understand why someone so beautiful, so loving, and so giving was stripped from our lives in an instant. The violent attack that Liora suffered has left a blistering anguish in our gut. Some will throw themselves into meaningless activity to fill a void left in the wake of her passing. That sadness we feel now is a sign that we are feeling Liora's presence, her love, her life and her loss."

When the service was over, they exited to a mass of photographers waiting outside. The location of the cemetery was not disclosed to the public out of respect for those invited to attend a private graveside burial. The casket was escorted by pallbearers and gently placed into a hearse waiting outside the funeral home. A police escort guaranteed that no paparazzi or on-lookers followed the funeral procession to the cemetery.

It was a crisp winter morning in Arlington. The dew was present on the blades of grass. Today was one of those days in your life when you wish you didn't have to live it. Saying goodbye is hard, it is heart wrenching, it is final.

Five layers deep family and friends stood at the burial site to bid their final farewell. Tears were flowing as the geese flew overhead marking the gray sky's exit into spring. It wouldn't be long now.

The four women stood shoulder to shoulder, more leaning than standing to keep from falling down. The echo of the minister resounded softly in their heads as they tried to take in why they were there. "God, give me strength," they all thought, "strength to get through the next minute." They couldn't think any farther ahead than one minute at a time. It was just too much to take in, too much to believe. They kept hoping if they closed their eyes tight enough when they opened again, it would all be a horrible mistake; a nightmare.

"It's time," Sheila whispered. "Everyone else is gone and we can't put this off any longer."

They joined hands to proceed to the coffin before it was lowered into the ground. One . . . two . . . three . . . four . . . five, they all fell atop the coffin; a rainbow of lilies, full of color indicative of new life. One might say it was the beginning of new life for her; everlasting life with no more pain, no more threats and no more fears.

They walked away arm-in-arm, tears streaming down their faces knowing it was the end for her, for the five of them, for *Quei Forti*. They got into the limousine waiting to take them back to the City.

"Driver, can you drop us at *The Gathering* please, 17th and L?" requested Sheila.

The ride from Arlington to Washington was riddled with silence. Words don't ever seem to do any good at a time like this. So they retreated into their own thoughts and tried to recall the vibrancy that was always part of who she was in life. They owed her a tribute to befit the life they shared. They needed to replace the sadness with the laughter of her soul that they'd all come to know and love. She was the glue that held them together. She was their voice of reason when they wanted to go off half-cocked, leaping before thinking and acting with caution abandoned. *Quei Forti* would never be the same. They lost the strongest link in the chain and had to learn how to rebuild.

The opening of the car door pulled them back to reality. "*The Gathering*, ladies. Will you be requiring my services anymore today?"

"No John," Sheila declined. "Thank you for your kindness. We can make it on our own from here."

"Hello ladies," greeted the bartender as they headed to their favorite spot in the back of the pub. "I've been expecting you today. Take a seat and I'll send your drinks to the table."

Sheila leaned in to place a slight kiss on his cheek. "The flowers were beautiful, Mickey. Thank you."

"Everyone here loved her, too. It's a sad day," he sorrowfully acknowledged.

They gathered around their favorite table in the back by the jukebox. Liora loved music and needed to be close to the songs. A small fortune was spent in the jukebox because the mood had to be high and the beat had to be up. They stared at the empty chair where she would have been sitting, another reminder that all of their lives were about to change. Nothing would ever be the same.

Cassie was the first to speak, "Hey, do you guys remember one of the first times we came here, the night Mickey was trying out a new band and their lead singer was late for the first set? Liora felt so bad for the band she jumped up on stage and filled in until their singer finally arrived."

Laughter sprang from each of them as they remembered her nervousness. Her voice was cracking until she looked over at them and gained the confidence she needed. Then the most beautiful sounds emerged from her mouth as she settled down to please the crowd.

"And do you remember . . . ?" Sunny abruptly stopped. She couldn't believe her eyes. "Is my mind playing tricks on me?" she thought to herself. Emerging from the back room was Lieutenant Marcello and standing behind him in the hallway was . . . "Impossible! She's dead!" she kept thinking.

Emily broke her thoughts, "Sunny what is it?"

Without changing her line of sight, Sunny lifted her hand and pointed in the direction of her vision. The vision moved closer until standing before her was Antonia Liora Courtlandt in the flesh. Liora reached out and embraced Sunny.

"Are you real?" she whispered.

"I am real," Liora confirmed.

Cassie rushed to embrace Liora, to feel her flesh and be sure she was real. Emily did not move. Staring at Sheila, who apparently was not surprised by Liora's presence, Emily was paralyzed by the shock, anger and betrayal consuming her at that moment.

Realizing she had to explain, Sheila took Emily's hand in hers. "There was no other way Honey. We couldn't chance too many people knowing and giving it away at the funeral."

"You mean you were in on this?" asked Cassie. "What the hell is going on?

Emily remained silent and tears were rolling down her cheeks.

"Please don't be angry with Sheila," Liora begged. "She didn't want to go along with the deception but Lieutenant Marcello and I convinced her it was the only way to catch Brent. The night he attacked me I almost died. Lieutenant Marcello was not lying when he told you my heart stopped twice in the ambulance on the way to the hospital. But the paramedics were able to revive me and because of their quick action and refusal to give up, I'm here today with all of you."

"I'm so sorry," mouthed Sheila to Emily.

"Emily," Liora continued, "we had to make Brent think I was dead. It was the only way to flush him out and force him to make a mistake. Lieutenant Marcello believed that if he thought I was dead, he would come to the funeral to witness his handy work. We needed Sheila to play along since she already knew what he looked like."

Emily broke her silence. "I know Brent Barea. I can identify Brent Barea. Why did you have to lie to all of us? You let us think you were dead. We grieved for you." Glaring at Sheila, she added, "And you knew all along."

"Because the more people that knew what we were doing, the greater the chance someone would tip him off," Liora explained. "We needed him to think it was real. We needed everyone at the funeral focused on my coffin. We couldn't chance that anyone checking out the crowd might make him suspicious."

"Was it worth putting your friends through all of this?" she angrily asked. "Did you get what you were after?"

"As a matter of fact we did," confirmed Lieutenant Marcello. "We got him. He's in custody right now and he won't be getting near any of you for the rest of his life."

"But how?" asked Cassie.

Sheila fielded that question. "We came up with a signal to indicate if I saw Brent among the mourners. At first there was no sign of him. But as the crowd thinned out and we approached the casket, I saw him standing in the background trying to be inconspicuous."

"When Sheila dropped two lilies instead of one, she told us he was there watching you all say goodbye," Lieutenant Marcello admitted. "He had to believe he got away with it. After you all left the cemetery, Brent approached the casket and that's when we arrested him."

"Is he saying anything?" asked Emily. "Did he tell you why he did this?"

"I didn't get a chance to interrogate him yet," he replied, "but when we were putting him in the patrol car, he said something about taking something from you that you took from him. Do you have any idea what that means?"

"If I had to guess," Emily began, "he loved me and believes I was taken from him so maybe he wanted to take someone from me that I loved."

"Maybe," he agreed. "Well, I need to get back to the station and take care of our prisoner. I'm sure you ladies have some celebrating to do."

Still finding it hard to believe, they repeatedly hugged Liora ensuring she was real.

"*Quei Forti* lives again!" announced Cassie.

"Well not exactly," corrected Sheila.

"What now?" asked Sunny.

"Back in New Orleans I told you I was searching for my daughter," she reminded them. "The private investigator I hired found the man who helped me with the adoption, the man I was in love with all those years ago. He's in Las Vegas now."

"You're leaving us?" asked Liora. "But we all just got our lives back."

Sheila reached across the table and took all of their hands in hers stating, "It is hard to move away from friends. This will be the second hardest thing I've ever had to do but I need your help. We built quality, enriching bonds and I'll take my experiences with each of you wherever I go. Remember the happy times and let the bad ones go. The countdown has started for the fall fashion show. You can start there. It will remind you of the good times. There are so many things about my past that I'd like to forget but she's not one of them. I gave away my heart a long time ago. It's time to find my daughter."

Edwards Brothers Malloy
Thorofare, NJ USA
February 3, 2015